W9-BTR-667

Llewellyn's

2018 Witches' Companion

An Almanac for Everyday Living

Llewellyn's 2018 Witches' Companion

ISBN 978-0-7387-3775-1

© Llewellyn Publications, Woodbury, Minnesota, USA. All rights reserved. No part of this book may be used or reproduced in any manner whatsoever, including Internet usage, without written permission from Llewellyn Worldwide Ltd., except for brief quotations embodied in critical articles or reviews.

Art Director: Lynne Menturweck
Cover art © Tim Foley
Cover designer: Lynne Menturweck
Designer: Joanna Willis
Editor: Andrea Neff

Interior illustrations:
Kathleen Edwards: 12, 15, 43, 47, 48, 85, 87, 121, 124, 127, 156, 160, 189, 192, 225, 228
Tim Foley: 9, 19, 22, 53, 56, 58, 83, 103, 104, 107, 131, 134, 145, 165, 169, 197, 200, 203, 235, 236
Bri Hermanson: 35,36, 111, 112, 116, 181, 184
Jennifer Hewitson: 27, 28, 31, 62, 67, 68, 91, 94, 99, 139, 142, 174, 177, 206, 211, 241, 246
Rik Olson: 73, 76, 79, 148, 152, 216, 221, 251, 253

Additional illustrations: Llewellyn Art Department

Any Internet references contained in this work are current at publication time, but the publisher cannot guarantee that a specific location will continue to be maintained.

You can order Llewellyn annuals and books from *New Worlds*, Llewellyn's magazine catalog. To request a free copy of the catalog, call toll-free 1-877-NEW-WRLD or visit our website at http://www.llewellyn.com.

Llewellyn Worldwide Ltd.
2143 Wooddale Drive
Woodbury, MN 55125-2989
www.llewellyn.com

Printed in the United States of America

Contents

Community Forum

Provocative Opinions on Contemporary Topics

Witchy Living

Day-by-Day Witchcraft

Witchcraft Essentials

Practices, Rituals & Spells

Magical Transformations

Everything Old Is New Again

The Lunar Calendar

September 2017 to December 2018

Community Forum

Provocative Opinions on Contemporary Topics

Chasing the Bunny: Why We Should Welcome Newcomers to the Craft

Charlynn Walls

We often think of Witchcraft and Wicca as being fairly inclusive spiritual paths. There are Pagan Pride days and festivals around the globe that enable us to come together and celebrate who we are. We hope to present a positive and welcoming image to those seeking a new path, and the majority of the time that is the case.

However, when we perceive that someone is not as serious about their spirituality as we think they should be, we sometimes deem them to be a "fluffy bunny." This derogatory term is most often thrown at those who are young in years or in spirit, and may not be based on anything more. It can also be utilized for those who have been seen as dabbling in the Craft.

Those who are exploring a new path may not be fully committed, and nor should they be until they are sure that this is where their heart is. But what they do bring with them in their pursuit is a fresh outlook, overwhelming enthusiasm, and a sense of wonder. So why are we so hard on those coming into the Craft?

We Have All Been There

At one time, each and every one of us was new to the path. It takes courage to begin a new venture, as you are never entirely sure what the outcome will be. There is a lot of uncertainty that surrounds one's newfound interest, and it often leaves one with more questions than answers. Each of us took our time, did research, became comfortable with our newly solidified spirituality, and then started reaching out to others in the pursuit of community. There was a feeling that we had finally come home. We probably had moments when we received positive feedback. We have also probably all been shot down at one time or another.

Our experiences entering our path helped to shape our outlook on Paganism. I, personally, was solitary for the longest time. This was because when I reached out to others, I was met with silence, or I was told that I needed to study more or did not have enough experience. I had a difficult time understanding how I could gain experience when no one would give me a moment of their time. I, like many newcomers, became frustrated that my search was in vain.

I can be a stubborn person at times. Because this was something important to me, I started working to prove myself. Since I place a high value on education, I dug in and studied. I read everything I could get

my hands on and went to classes at local shops. I was persistent and kept trying. I continued to try to reach out to those around me.

It was still very hard to get a response from people in my local area. Fortunately, I moved soon after my journey began and was able to land in a community where people were more receptive and welcoming. They met my enthusiasm equally and provided ways for me to become involved. They even helped steer me toward community service. In my new community, my awe was seen as an asset rather than something detrimental. That perspective enabled me to have conversations with peers and elders alike. They shared their experiences and we were richer for having discussed our similarities and differences.

Supporting One Another

Almost every day I come across an email from someone who is searching, whether it is for information or community. I take those emails as an opportunity to do for someone what I would have liked to have been done for me when I was just starting out. So I take a moment to respond. You would be surprised how much such a simple act affects people.

Many people who are new to the Craft have been met with silence or have been disregarded outright. I do believe that anyone who is just starting out should have a good foundational knowledge, and I will often recommend several books for them to read. However, a person can only read so many books. The information in them is invaluable, but so is interaction with someone who has been walking the path. A book cannot have a conversation with you or provide you with additional insights into something that has caught your interest. I am also aware that groups rarely extend an invitation to a seeker without some prior knowledge of how the person interacts with others and how they behave in a group setting.

Knowing my local community gives me a way to provide novices with information on how to come into contact with people who could enhance and help them on their journey. I often recommend that the person contacting me get out and meet people. In my local area there are often discussion groups that meet, along with open full moon and dark moon celebrations where people of various pathways can share their knowledge or participate in ritual. I take note of when and where these activities occur and who facilitates them. I want to point people in the correct direction but also toward activities that will be public and nonthreatening.

In order to cultivate positive magickal experiences, we have to be willing to put ourselves out there for people and work with others. We need to create places where people are free to explore the possibilities available to them. The more positive experiences that we can create for a new person, the more likely they will be to commit to their path and to be able to deal with times of stagnation and frustration.

There will be some people, of course, who decide that this path is not for them. That is natural and is to be expected. For those who decide to move on, hopefully their time of exploration was filled with positive experiences that they can relate to others. For those who do decide to take the next step and dedicate themselves to the path, you will have provided the scaffolding for a well-rounded practitioner, solitary or not.

Chasing the Bunny

Seasoned practitioners are often faced with disillusionment and burnout from involvement in community activities and groups that they run or take part in. There are also those who have faced a crisis of faith and have come out the other side. Some of the fun and excitement of the Craft may have dissipated, but they are firmly rooted in their path. They take their commitment to their path seriously and want others to be just as sincere. So they often mistakenly think all newcomers are lackadaisical in their approach.

The thing is, we all strive to get back to those moments of pure joy in our practice. We long for the moments when we experience something profound and affirming. These are the attributes that come easily to the novice who comes into things with fresh eyes and a fresh perspective.

I often wonder if the reason that we are so hard on those whom we think lack experience is really more about ourselves than about them. I do not think that it is simply jealousy on the part of the seasoned practitioner that makes them hesitant or has them lashing out. I believe that it has more to do with an inability to adequately connect, perhaps due to becoming jaded or becoming overwhelmed by the daily grind of life.

What we want is to once again experience the astonishment when a spell or ritual works beyond our expectations, to once again hold the deep reverence we once had when we enjoyed a moment of communion with our deities or simply out in nature. We need to embrace those who are new, because through them we are afforded the chance to experience such moments again. Those moments are infectious and allow us to return to a simpler time in our lives when everything held wonder for us.

I am reminded of my attendance at a ritual during one of my first festivals. There were several of us who had started our paths into the community at the same time, and we were like a close-knit family. We were thrilled at the prospect of participating in one of our first large rituals. The drumming felt like a pulse, and we became caught up in it. As we walked to the place where the ritual circle was, we were already entranced. The ritual spoke to us and we experienced energy on a new level. It seemed to build around us and provided a protective shield as it began to rain. Several of us remarked later that we had remained completely dry during the ritual even though the rain shower had been substantial. We talked and shared this experience with one another as well as those who had facilitated the ritual.

As you can imagine, we were ecstatic about what we had experienced together. How was it possible that others around us had been wet after the rain but we were dry? We talked excitedly about the possibilities, and it was just as affirming for those we talked with as it was for those who had experienced it. We were brimming with excitement. Through our enthusiasm, the others tapped into something that they thought they had lost. They experienced with us that moment of elation, and it brought back fond memories of their early days. It also had the added benefit of confirming for them that they really were making a difference and that their hard work was worth the effort.

Conclusions

There is a mutualistic symbiotic relationship between those who are new to the Craft and those who have been involved in it for a number of years. This is perhaps one of the greatest mysteries that is not often discussed in modern Paganism. Each of us brings a perspective that others can utilize in their own practice. We benefit from one another's insights and experiences. It is more than just an elder passing along information to the novice, though that is often how it is presented in books and movies.

Each moment has the potential for knowledge to be shared between both the novice and the seasoned practitioner. We can all learn from one another.

Each moment has the potential for knowledge to be shared between both the novice and the seasoned practitioner. We can all learn from one another. There was a time when our coven gathered at Samhain and we were relaxing around the fire after a particularly emotional ritual. A log in the fire suddenly started to spew a long, solid-blue flame. Another member and I looked at each other and we raised our eyebrows. We realized that we still had spiritual company from the ritual.

The other members were intrigued with the activity going on in the fire but did not realize what it meant. Since I was still relatively new to the group and many of them had been involved with Paganism for much longer, I was hesitant to share what I knew, even though these were women I considered family. We ended up discussing how this was an indication that the spirits we had invited to our rite had not taken the cue to leave at the appointed time, so we acknowledged our visitors and then firmly asked them to go. In that moment, we were able to share knowledge, and it became a powerful teaching moment for all of us.

Experience is also a powerful motivator. It is ultimately what determines if we will continue with an activity or not. Our perspective of a ritual or spell is uniquely our own, but we can share what we have witnessed or felt. We form strong connections through shared experiences. The women in circle that evening will always remember what we shared and what we learned from each other.

So while someone may be new to the Craft, they do still have knowledge and experiences to share with us that are invaluable. It would behoove us to be open to what they have to offer and reserve judgment on their intentions. After all, if we do not, then who is really the fluffy bunny in the situation?

Charlynn Walls *resides with her family in central Missouri. She holds a* BA *in anthropology, with an emphasis in archaeology. She is acting* CEO *of* Correllian Education Ministries, *which oversees* Witch School. *She is an active member of the* St. Louis Pagan *community and is part of a local area coven. Charlynn teaches by presenting at various local festivals on a variety of topics. She continues to pursue her writing through articles for* Witches & Pagans *magazine, several* Llewellyn *annuals, and her blog,* Sage Offerings, *at www.sageofferings.net.*

Illustrator: Kathleen Edwards

How to Be a Magical Friend

James Kambos

If you're a magical person, you know that a great deal of responsibility comes with walking a magical path. You must be kind, caring, and ethical. You understand karma and know that our actions—positive or negative—will come back to us. As you live a magical life and as your skills in the magical arts begin to grow, many people, magical and non-magical, will seek you out to help them with their lives. That's why it's important to learn how to be what I call a "magical friend."

Sometimes the only thing a person needs from you is someone to lean on and someone who will listen. But many times people will need your help handling complex issues in their lives. The idea for this article came about because I think magical folk need to be prepared for the people and situations they may encounter along the way. This is my story. Your story may be different.

You don't need to be a high priestess or a practicing Witch to develop a following of dedicated individuals who will come to you for magical help and advice. If you have psychic abilities or talents in using the tarot, regular playing cards, or a pendulum, you will be in demand. People will also beat a path to your door if you're known for scrying.

This all reminds me of my childhood growing up in the hills of Appalachia. Almost every backcountry village or hollow had their own psychic, card reader, or conjurer. Most communities had someone who had the gift of "second sight," who could tell your fortune. I can remember visiting some of these "seers" and having to wait on the front porch because so many other people were ahead of me. As I recall, their predictions were usually extremely accurate. They were able to help people with financial/business concerns and, of course, matters of the heart. They could tell you if your husband was still seeing that redhead, and they knew what *really* happened to that boy who disappeared down by the coal mine last winter.

If you have similar skills, be prepared to be a psychic counselor-confidant-friend.

It's in the Cards

When I was still in college, I visited one of these backwoods-country card readers. Her reading and predictions were right on target. I was hooked. I knew this was something I wanted to do. Soon after, while standing in a slow-moving supermarket checkout line, something caught my eye. It was an inexpensive paperback titled *How to Tell Fortunes with Playing Cards.*

That was my turning point. I bought it and read it cover to cover. I did a few spreads for myself. Then I called a friend and did a reading for him. He sat across from me on the floor of my apartment. With each prediction his eyes got wider. I wanted to stop because I thought I was way off, but he told me to keep going.

Before I knew it, my friend came back with a friend. The same thing happened. Soon, on most Saturdays, friends were stopping by for card readings and my magical "career" was launched.

Over the years I expanded my talents and began using tarot cards and a pendulum, also with good results.

I've Got a Secret

In fact, I've got *lots* of secrets, and if you begin to do any magical work for others, you'll have quite a few, too. My best advice to you is to *keep your mouth shut.* If you really want to be a helpful magical friend, you must learn to keep what you're told by those seeking your help confidential. This is one of the greatest responsibilities you'll have as a magical friend.

Not only is it unkind to spread gossip, but it will also hurt your reputation. On top of that, the more you talk about your magic, the more you'll weaken the results.

I've had people come to me for card consultations who were having extramarital affairs and anything else you could imagine, but I always keep it to myself. Now, don't get me wrong: if my reading shows that person is headed for big trouble, believe me, I tell them. What they do with the information I give them is their business.

When dealing with someone else's personal life, you should feel flattered that they trust you enough to confide in you. Never betray that trust, and never judge anyone.

Love Me, Love Me Not

Love. Falling in love. Falling out of love.

If there is one aspect of the human condition that will bring people to you seeking magical help more than anything else, it's love. I have probably done more card readings and pendulum consultations for people in love, falling in love, and falling out of love than for anything else.

If there is one aspect of the human condition that will bring people to you seeking magical help more than anything else, it's love. I have probably done more card readings and pendulum consultations for people in love, falling in love, and falling out of love than for anything else.

Here are some points to remember when doing magical work for those dealing with love. First, love is blind. You, as a magical friend, may think to yourself, *What do they see in that scumbag?* Remember, don't judge; just do what you're asked. Second, don't sugarcoat any kind of answer you see in a love reading of any kind. Give it to 'em straight. Third—and this is a biggie—don't cast any love spells involving a specific person! A love spell directed

VI
THE LOVERS.

at a specific person is a form of manipulation and can lead to some disastrous karmic consequences. So no love spells to bring a specific person into someone's life should ever be performed, by you or the seeker, no matter how much they beg. Also, please warn the person seeking love to avoid any online spellcasters dealing in love magic.

While we're on the subject of love, be aware that love is probably the one thing that can make people needy and dependent. Be careful if someone begins to become too dependent on you and asks for too much magical help. There was one woman who used to come to me several times a week for tarot readings concerning her love life. I told her that the readings were very strong and that I didn't see her situation changing for about two or three months. I had to urge her to stop coming to me so frequently and to ride things out.

If this type of situation happens to you, explain to the individual that magic and divination should be empowering. A reading should prepare someone to make wise choices on their own; it shouldn't make them dependent on you.

Love magic can put you, the magical friend, in an awkward position. My best advice here is to keep in mind that it's okay to occasionally give someone a glimpse into the future of their love life, using your favorite divination tool, but don't let them turn it into a crutch.

Spellbound

I hear it all the time: "Can you put a spell on my spouse/boss/neighbor?"

Yes, I could, but I won't. Spellwork for friends can get you into an uncomfortable situation. First of all, you may not clearly understand their goal. Also, you probably won't have the same energy as they do about the matter, so the results won't be the same. Most importantly, if the spell doesn't work, it's going to be *your* fault.

What you can do is direct them to books about spellcasting. Llewellyn, for example, has a great line of spell books for all skill levels. Suggest that they learn to cast their own spell and you could coach them. Add that it will be more effective that way.

I'd hate to see a relationship go sour because a spell didn't work. That's why I don't do spells for someone else.

Dollars and Cents

Should you charge for your services as a soothsayer, diviner, or magical friend? I can't answer for you, but I don't. I don't think I should charge a friend, and I just enjoy doing it.

But if you decide to do this sort of thing full-time and it's your means of making a living, then of course charge for your services. Just be sure to follow your state and local business ordinances.

Even if you don't charge, I see nothing wrong with accepting a small gift in exchange for a reading. Now and then, after doing quite a few readings/consultations for certain people, I've been given a pound of gourmet coffee or fine chocolate.

Spread the Magic

Living a magical life is a powerful way to live. Being a magical friend to those in need adds to that power. When people come to you to ask your advice and you help them see what their future may hold, you empower them. You have it in your power to help people make wise choices. Go ahead—spread the magic!

James Kambos *writes and paints from his home in the beautiful hill country of southern Ohio. He learned about magic by watching his Greek grandmother perform folk magic spells that she brought from Greece. He graduated from Ohio University.*

Illustrator: Tim Foley

Exonerating the Warlock: A Brief History & Revisioning of a Misunderstood Term

Storm Faerywolf

To those who are outside the Neo-Pagan movement, I am usually labeled a *Warlock*. As a man who is also a practitioner of Witchcraft, I don't find this surprising, since English dictionaries are fairly unanimous in defining this word as "a male witch or sorcerer," and have done so for half a millennia. Numerous works of poetry and literature spanning hundreds of years have used the term in this manner. It's only when you move inside the Neo-Pagan bubble that this word suddenly becomes problematic.

To some modern practitioners, *Warlock* is thought of as an insult. Early Neo-Pagan writers—likely in an effort to promote the idea that they were in possession of a special type of insider knowledge—asserted that since *Warlock* derived from an older word with an arguably negative meaning, the term was rarely if ever used by actual Witches. While their observations of the word's origins were correct, they failed to take into consideration the cultural context of those origins, or even basic rules of language.

Let me take this moment to proudly affirm: I am a Warlock. Though attitudes are slowly changing, when I'm addressing an audience of other Witches and Pagan folk, this revelation is often met with judgment and even disdain. Even you, dear reader, may have already formed an opinion about who I am or what I do based on my decision to self-identify with this term. Believe me when I say I have probably heard it all: "Warlock means 'oath breaker.' You obviously don't know what you are doing." "Warlocks are those who have betrayed their coven! Why would you use that term?" "You must be new to the Craft. No experienced or self-respecting Witch would use that word."

Let me take this moment to proudly affirm: I am a Warlock. Though attitudes are slowly changing, when I'm addressing an audience of other Witches and Pagan folk, this revelation is often met with judgment and even disdain.

Though such people are grossly misinformed, I can't exactly blame them. This is because early practitioners of the modern Craft, either mistakenly or deliberately, misrepresented the term. While *warlock* does likely derive from an older word that originally

meant "one that breaks faith,"[1] its Christian-era origin must be taken into account when considering this application. Before the year 900 CE, the Old English *wǣrloga* (from which the modern Scottish *warlock* derives) was used to mean someone who had broken his baptismal covenant.[2] During the forced Christianization of Western Europe, country folk were often made to swear allegiance to the new Church, which included renouncing their previous religious observances. Men who continued to practice what was then considered by the Church to be heresy were sometimes branded "warlocks." In other words, the word was used to describe men whom today we might identify as *Pagan* (another term with an older, originally negative meaning that has been reclaimed in recent times).

Though scholars accept the "male Witch" definition of Warlock as being correct, some Neo-Pagan circles have dug in their heels and have even expanded upon the original meaning, asserting that it *really* means "a Witch who betrays their coven." There is, however, no historical evidence of this usage prior to the 1950s, meaning that the origin of this folk belief is a modern reinterpretation, and one that was (again, either deliberately or mistakenly) used to promote those in the Pagan movement as having special knowledge of the subject—knowledge

1. While the Oxford English Dictionary continues to dismiss alternative etymologies (such as the Norse *vardlokur*, which refers to a singer of enchanted songs), there is growing evidence for an etymology outside of the commonly accepted Old English root. For one example, see the definition of *warlock* in Samuel Johnson's 1755 classic A *Dictionary of the English Language*, http://johnsonsdictionaryonline.com/?p=5185.

2. Rev. Abram Smythe Palmer, *Folk-Etymology* (London: George Bell and Sons, 1882), 426.

that, upon further examination, evaporates into thin air. And yet, even in the face of these facts, the problem persists.

The misconception of the meaning of the word *warlock* is a prime example of the *etymological fallacy*,[3] which is when a word's previous definition or root (an *etymon*) is incorrectly assumed to be that word's "true" meaning without regard to how words evolve and change definition over time (aka *semantic shift*). Consider the English word *decimate*, which means "to destroy a large portion of." This word derives from the Latin *decimāre*, meaning "to destroy (or punish) one of every ten." Because of its original meaning, some assert that the word decimate *really* means to destroy only one-tenth of something—that is, until an etymologist comes along and ruins their argument with those pesky *facts*.

3. R. L. G., "The Etymological Fallacy," *The Economist* (Aug. 2, 2011), www.economist.com/blogs/johnson/2011/08/word-origins-and-meaning.

While it might be academically interesting to cite a word's previous etymons, it would be incorrect to assume that they somehow reveal the true meaning of a word. This simply isn't how language works. Plenty of words have different or even opposite meanings today than how they were originally used. Consider *gay* (originally meaning "having or showing a merry, lively mood"), *brave* ("cowardice"), or even *girl* ("a child of either sex").[4] The list goes on and on. Language does not exist in a static state, and therefore older definitions do not have any bearing on that word's current usage or definition.

Even *Pagan*—a word much used in our community to refer to a person who practices their religion or spirituality outside of the monotheistic faiths—was originally a type of insult. From the Latin *paganus*, meaning "country dweller," it was used in the pre-Christian Roman era to mean something like "civilian, incompetent soldier."[5] It would have been applied to those who lived outside of cities and was used as a pejorative, such as some might use *hick* or *redneck* today.

Moving forward with the awareness that the prejudice against the word *warlock* is based on nothing more than a linguistic misunderstanding, one might think that more people would at least be open to embracing the term. But old habits die hard, it seems.

Another argument against the use of this word in the modern Craft is its gender specificity. *Warlock* is traditionally masculine. It has been suggested that the use of a gender-specific term such as this seeks to divide our community rather than unify it. To this I must respectfully but unequivocally disagree. Aside from the fact that we already have gender-specific terms in the Craft (as many a High Priestess can certainly attest), there is no reason that the adoption of an identifying term specific to any subgroup needs to invalidate the identities of any

4. Maria Boomhower, "Etymology: How Words Change Over Time," EzineArticles.com (Feb. 2, 2005), http://ezinearticles.com/?-Etymology–How-Words-Change-Over-Time &id=12709.

5. Online Etymology Dictionary, s.v. "pagan," www.etymonline.com/index.php?term=pagan.

others. Labels can no doubt divide us when they are applied to others. But when a group decides to adopt one for themselves, it is an act of both self-reflection and communal empowerment, much as was done with the words *gay*, *lesbian*, and *Witch*.

In the United States, *Witch* became not only a spiritual and magical identifier but also a term with political importance. When Starhawk wrote *The Spiral Dance* in 1979, she popularized the idea of modern practitioners using the term as a means to consciously identify with those unfortunate (mostly female) individuals who, during the 300-year period between the fifteenth and eighteenth centuries, were accused, imprisoned, tortured, and killed for the "crime" of Witchcraft. Though these poor souls were almost certainly *not* Witches (but instead ill-fated Christians who had the misfortune of falling on the bad side of their church or local government), by making an association with those falsely accused we stand united against a mindset that would seek to make the pursuit of the magical arts a criminal act. *Witch* became a rallying cry for all who would stand against an oppressive system, whether that system was one of religious faith, governmental dominance, or societal coercion.

While an excellent case has been made for the term *Witch* being gender-neutral (and both history and common use will support this), it cannot be denied that the word has definitive feminine connotations. Its origins (the Old English *wicce*) as well as its current definition both refer specifically to women. If you asked ten people off the street to describe a Witch, you would be hard-pressed to find *one* who would do so in anything but female terms. Witchcraft, plain and simple, is a female-dominated practice, and as such it stands against the current societal norm on this notion alone.

But why just men? Why weren't women usually labeled as *Warlocks* for the heresy of Witchcraft? The *Malleus Maleficarum* ("The Hammer of Witches," 1487) was instrumental in promoting a gender-skewed view of Witchcraft. The practice was seen as the demonic exploitation

of what was believed to be an inherent feminine weakness, as women were thought to be more susceptible than men to the influence of the devil, just as Eve was thought to have been susceptible to the serpent in the Garden of Eden. Though the gender statistics are nearly reversed in Eastern Europe,[6] in Western European countries those accused of the crime of Witchcraft were overwhelmingly women. Witchcraft, in the popular mindset, was firmly established as a woman's art, and this mentality has been handed down in English-speaking countries ever since.

Though purely speculative on my part, this observation could also shed some light on how the term *Warlock* might have first been applied, or at least add a nuance to our understanding of how that term came about to specifically describe men, rather than women, accused

6. Dan Lohr, "Cultural Distinction in the Witch Hunts of Russia," Washington and Lee University, http://witchhunts.academic.wlu.edu/cultural-distinction-in-the-witch-hunts-of-russia.

of practicing the "dark arts." Since Witchcraft in the West was seen as being a particularly feminine phenomena, those men who would engage in such "womanly" arts were breaking what was considered to be a sacred covenant: that of the supposed divine supremacy of men over women. A Warlock had left the sanctuary of the patriarchal Church and instead cavorted with the devil and womenfolk. It was an insult in part because it was *emasculating.* In a patriarchal world in which perceived masculinity is vitally important as well as exceedingly fragile, there can be no greater fear for a man than to have his "male credentials" summarily revoked.

While many men today are quite comfortable embracing the term *Witch* (and rightly so!), there are others who wish to make a case for exploring what can be thought of as "male mysteries" within the Craft. While an examination of these mysteries is beyond the scope of this piece, it should be understood that there are many types of male mysteries, just as there are many different ways to be a man.

Whether or not my previous speculation is factually true, in terms of a poetic truth and the living nature of language, it becomes part of a new understanding of how we can approach the modern use of the word *Warlock,* should we choose to identify with the term. This approach is one that is not just used to carve out a specific identity for men in the Craft but also speaks of rejecting both the patriarchal oppression of women and the idea that behaviors and inherent value are determined by one's gender. Warlocks are the gender-bending, gender-equality-minded men of Witchcraft who, by stepping outside of the boxes and narrow definitions provided by the overculture, gain power and insight that many "straightlaced" men will never know.

In terms of a title of power, *Warlock* accomplishes for men what *Witch* did for women. It gives us a particular point around which we can rally that both encourages our power to stand up to society and affirms our own gender. For men in the Craft, this can be an especially potent tool in rethinking what it means to be "masculine," with the hope of redefining masculinity to include many different types of behavioral expressions. Under this banner, we affirm that we are prepared to embrace the full spectrum of what it means to be a man who practices the "womanly" arts of Witchcraft, that we are not afraid to be vulnerable and also be warriors, and healers, and educators, and lovers at the same time.

Warlock is a word of power, and as such it will evoke different feelings for different people. No one should feel compelled to begin adopting it, if they are firmly against it. But neither should anyone assert that it is *wrong* to use this word, for little more reason than because they misunderstand how language works. To do so demeans not only the English language but also the memory of those who dared (and continue to dare) to defy the pressure to stay inside their societally sanctioned boxes and fully embrace what it means to be a brother of the art.

Storm Faerywolf *is a professional author, teacher,* Warlock, *and co-owner of the* Mystic Dream, *a spiritual supply and bookstore where he teaches and offers magical services to the public. An initiate of the Faery tradition with over thirty years' experience practicing* Witchcraft, *he has been teaching magic and spirituality both privately and publicly for more than twenty years. He holds the* Black Wand *of a* Faery Master *and is the founder of his own lineage of the tradition,* BlueRose, *which offers extensive personal training both in person and online. He is the author of* Betwixt & Between: Exploring the Faery Tradition of Witchcraft *and* The Stars Within the Earth. *He is a founding teacher of the* Black Rose Witchcraft *online school and travels internationally teaching the magical arts. For more information, visit his website at* Faerywolf.com.

Illustrator: Jennifer Hewitson

Worshipping Widely and Cultural Appropriation

Deborah Blake

When I was a kid, maybe nine or ten or so, I went through a period of time when I thought Native Americans were incredibly cool. They are, of course—just not in the simplistic way I looked at them back then. Mind you, when I was studying them in school, they were still referred to as Indians, so that gives you some idea of how long ago it was. My point is, I was so enamored with their culture that I spent the better part of a year wearing my long dark-brown hair in braids and telling everyone I was Native American. That, alas, was not so cool. Still, I was nine. I can probably be excused.

These days, we'd call that *cultural appropriation*. And unless you're nine, someone is probably going to call you on it sooner or later.

Cultural appropriation, at its most basic level, is when someone adopts aspects of a culture that is not their own. The concept is considerably more complicated than that, however, and has special relevance when it comes to modern Witchcraft and Neopaganism, in which many of us follow a path that strays far from our own origins. Can we worship deities and integrate practices not from our particular cultural background without it becoming cultural appropriation?

While there are those who might disagree with me, I would argue that it is almost impossible *not* to use parts of other cultures in a modern Witchcraft practice, at least for some of us, and it all comes down to attitude and approach.

One very simple example is the use of sage smudge sticks for cleansing and clearing the energy of a person and/or space. This is a practice adapted from Native American roots, and yet it is now an integral part of many magical and spiritual rites. I use it on a regular basis just to clear away the "sludge" of daily life, and it is how my group, Blue Moon Circle, has started every ritual we've done together for over a dozen years. I can't imagine not using sage. But if you want to get technical, this practice could be considered cultural appropriation.

A much more complicated issue concerns deity/deities. For many, modern Witchcraft is a polytheistic religion, involving the worship of more than one god/goddess, often from more than one culture. Over the years, Blue Moon Circle has consisted of a number of different women who worship different deities. Sometimes we use the general term "God and Goddess" when invoking deity in circle, and sometimes, depending on the sabbat, the time of year, who is leading the ritual, or the intent of whichever spell we are working, we might call on someone specific. Brigid and Hecate and Demeter, the Horned

God and Apollo...they have all been called upon in turn. Hecate, in particular, is my patron goddess, the one who called to me the loudest.

None of them are the gods or goddesses from my culture of origin.

You see, I was brought up Jewish. And while I am very proud of my Jewish heritage, I never connected with the patriarchal god figure of my youth. But in theory, if I were to avoid any issues of cultural appropriation, I would be limited to worshipping that god (sorry...God). There was only one. And you have to go *really* far back to find anything resembling a goddess figure.

Some folks might say, "Well, your people were Russian Jews and Polish Jews, so you should stick to the gods from those cultures." The problem with this argument is that the Jews were never considered to be part of those cultures, even if they might have worn the same clothes or cooked some of the same foods as their neighbors. So if I'm not allowed to worship a deity from outside of the culture I was born into, I'm kind of stuck with that One God.

And no insult to the folks for whom that works, but I really needed to connect with Goddess. Lots of goddesses, and a few gods, but most especially with Hecate.

She's another interesting example of how difficult it can be to stick to one particular culture. Most people think of Hecate (or Hekate) as a Greek goddess, but she probably originated in Anatolia, a part of Asia Minor located in Turkey. She was worshipped by the Egyptians and Romans and in much of Europe throughout the centuries. So does she belong to only one culture or many? Was it cultural appropriation when her worship spread across the continents? Is it okay to worship her now if you have ties to any of those cultures, or only with the Greek? Or the Turkish (if we want to get really technical)?

Many of the gods and goddesses held sacred by modern Witches have the same kind of multicultural span. Almost all of the Greek gods have Roman counterparts. Isis was worshipped not just in Egypt but also as far away as East Africa and into Western Asia and Europe. Whose culture does she belong to?

Of course, our connection to individual gods and goddesses often goes far beyond the issue of whether or not we follow a particular pantheon, such as Greek, Egyptian, or Celtic. For most of us, it was less a matter of choosing a god or goddess to address our prayers to than it was the realization that they had chosen *us*. If a god or goddess calls our name, should we ignore them because the culture they originated in is not the same as our own?

For most of us, it was less a matter of choosing a god or goddess to address our prayers to than it was the realization that they had chosen *us*. If a god or goddess calls our name, should we ignore them because the culture they originated in is not the same as our own?

I don't know about you, but I don't particularly want to explain that to Hecate. Something tells me it wouldn't go over well. Is it more disrespectful to use aspects of a culture not our own or to turn our backs on the sacred elements that call to our hearts and spirits? These are tough questions, and each of us must find the answers that are right for us.

One of the characteristics of modern Witchcraft that appealed to me the most was how open and flexible it was. I'd tried a number of different paths—Judaism, Unitarian Universalism, Buddhism, and Taoism—and nothing really resonated with me until I stood in my first magic circle, on Samhain, no less, and finally felt Someone reaching back when I reached out. On that night, God and Goddess didn't have a name; I just knew them for what they were. Later, after I'd studied and practiced extensively, I was able to pick and choose those aspects of an eclectic Witchcraft practice that worked the best for me.

Practicing Witchcraft changed my life forever, and much for the better, but none of those aspects came from my original cultural background. Not one.

This isn't something I ignore, nor do I take it for granted. Rather, I am fully aware of and grateful for the cultures whose beliefs and tools I have borrowed. I treat all my adopted practices with respect and would not use anything if I thought that doing so would in any way harm the original culture from which it came.

In short, I am not taking away *from*, but rather, I hope, adding *to* the great range of the human magical experience. While it is certainly true that there are those in the modern Witchcraft world who do not take their practice seriously, or whose use of pieces from other cultures is thoughtless or disrespectful, I don't believe that is the norm.

I think for most of us these gifts from other cultures are seen not as *other*, but rather as part of our shared magical heritage, no matter what our culture of origin might be. A friend of mine, a White woman, was *called* by Yemaya, an African goddess. This might seem odd to those who don't understand the strange ways that deity can move in our lives, but for her, it is not cultural appropriation; it is her faith. It is the path that the goddess herself invited her to walk.

This, for me, is at the very heart of this argument, when you ask if the practice of modern Witchcraft, with its use of so many gods and beliefs and tools of other cultures, is guilty of cultural appropriation. Certainly, in some cases and with some people, that is probably the case. But for most of us, we are simply listening to the gods when they whisper in our ears, and following our hearts down the paths that lead to our spiritual growth and happiness.

There is no careless theft here, not even the kind that a nine-year-old might unintentionally indulge in. There is respect and worship and faith, and in all the best possible ways there is a mingling of many cultures as we come together to celebrate that which has guided the human spirit for centuries.

Deborah Blake *is the award-winning author of* The Goddess Is in the Details, Everyday Witchcraft, *and numerous other books from* Llewellyn. *She has published many articles in* Llewellyn *annuals, and her ongoing column, "Everyday Witchcraft," is featured in* Witches & Pagans *magazine. Deborah is also the author of the paranormal romance* Baba Yaga *series from* Berkley Publishing, *as well as the* Veiled Magic *urban fantasies. Deborah can be found online at* Facebook, Twitter, *and www.deborahblakeauthor.com. She lives in a 130-year-old farmhouse in rural upstate* New York *with numerous cats who supervise all her activities, both magickal and mundane.*

Illustrator: Bri Hermanson

Freemasonry: The "Other" Craft

Raven Digitalis

When us witchy types hear the term *the Craft*, it usually brings to mind either the idea of Witchcraft itself or the awesome nineties film of the same name. But there's actually an earlier usage of the term: *the Craft of the Freemasons.*

Freemasonry, or Masonry for short, is one of the most historically influential organizations in the world. Often considered to be shrouded in secrecy (as well as the subject of some far-out conspiracy theories), the Masons are not actually a secret society but are instead a society that happens to have a few secrets.

As far as Masonic secrets are concerned, don't believe the hype. Virtually anything about the organization, including its secret words, grips, and gestures, can be researched on the Internet. Like many other initiated Masons, I personally don't see too much of a problem with this, because regardless of how many "secrets" are exposed online, they remain theoretical and empty of meaning. Perhaps these "exposed" secrets can be understood intellectually on some level, but this doesn't hold a candle to the actual *practice* of learning these codes within the paradigm of a loving fraternal brotherhood. Masonry is experiential, not merely theoretical.

Fascinating Foundations and Sanctified Symbolism

The Ancient Free and Accepted Masons (AFAM) is a fraternal order with numerous ties to occultism, even if many of the members claim otherwise. While the Masons are not specifically an occult order and are not a magickal tradition, they are indeed a global spiritual brotherhood with long-held traditions and solid codes of ethics.

As is the case in original Gardnerian Wicca, the Craft of the Masons consists of three primary degrees (called the Blue Lodge). Additionally, there are a number of optional "addendum" degrees expressed in the branches of the York Rite and the Scottish Rite. Masonry makes use of symbolism derived from ancient Egypt, Hermetic philosophy, alchemical principles, stories of the Knights Templar, the legend of King Solomon's Temple, numerous stories within the Bible, and many other ancient milieus. However, Freemasonry's origin is closer to 1700 CE and originates from the creative minds of medieval English and Scottish stonemasons. The United Grand Lodge of England was established in 1717. The "Free and Accepted" portion of the title is derived from this point in history, when ordinary men were permitted to join *operative* Masonic clubs (consisting of gentlemen working in building trades) around 1640. These non-operative Masons were

G

called *accepted* Masons because they were allowed to join the brotherhood of Scottish Masonic fraternities without necessarily having careers in "operative" building trades. In modern times, only a handful of initiated Masons have "operative" Masonic careers.

A well-known phrase used by Masons to describe the Craft is "Making good men better." Masonry's goal is to help men alchemize their mind and emotions through lessons, discourse, and brotherhood, helping refine a person's character into spiritual gold.

The Craft of the Freemasons utilizes countless occult symbols and philosophies, many of which have influenced modern-day Witchcraft. While I won't go into great detail about this in these pages, readers are welcome to research the numerous books and articles that examine Masonic symbolism in depth. Just be sure to keep away from the articles that discuss Satanic or Illuminati conspiracies. Masonic lodges are much more concerned with raising money for charity than with raising demons!

Readers are welcome to research the numerous books and articles that examine Masonic symbolism in depth. Just be sure to keep away from the articles that discuss Satanic or Illuminati conspiracies. Masonic lodges are much more concerned with raising money for charity than with raising demons!

Thousands of esoteric symbols are utilized in the Masonic Craft, each of which has its own nuanced meaning. Some of these symbols are strictly initiatory, while others are quite common. The Square and Compasses is easily the most well-known Masonic symbol and is found in all Masonic lodges around the world. The emblem is also common on virtually all "brotherly bling," such as rings, necklaces, pocket watches, compasses, pocket knives, bumper stickers, and so on. It is also a popular tattoo! The simple symbolism of the architectural square is to "square" our actions with virtuous conduct. The two interlocked compasses represent keeping our actions within "due bounds" (i.e., the restraint of immoral behaviors). During initiation, a Mason is given various meanings of the divine letter "G" that graces the inside of the symbol.

Another highly popular Masonic symbol is the Eye of Providence. In simplest terms, the Eye of Providence represents the Eye of God. (The "God" in this meaning is up to individual practitioners themselves—personally, I prefer to see it as the Eye of Shiva!) This symbol takes a multitude of forms and is commonly depicted atop a pyramid. Freemasonry utilizes a hefty amount of ancient Egyptian symbolism, and the pyramid is no exception. After all, could there be a better symbol of humankind's architectural genius?! The Eye of Providence and pyramid are, of course, famously depicted on the back of the American dollar bill. This certainly seems appropriate considering that many of the nation's Founding Fathers were Freemasons, including George Washington, Benjamin Franklin, and James Monroe.

Nonprofit Nobility and Divine Diversity

Masonry and its offshoots are social clubs. Not only that, but they are nonprofit organizations that perform a wide variety of civic and social work to raise funding and awareness for individuals in need, whether they be school kids, elderly folks, individuals with disabilities, and so on. Just look at the work of the Shriners, whose hospitals provide treatment to children with illnesses and injuries. (The Shriners are a separate club, and a prerequisite of membership is that one also be a Freemason. And while I personally do not support their circuses, their hospitals are something to be marveled at. The Shriners also wear tasseled red fez hats and drive mini "midget" cars in parades, which is equally fabulous!)

Freemasonry is historically a masculine brotherhood, though a number of Masonic appendant bodies (allied organizations) are predominantly female, such as the Order of the Eastern Star, Daughters of the Nile, and Job's Daughters International. Others are male-oriented, such as the Shriners and the Order of DeMolay, while some, such as the Rosicrucians, are co-ed. Traditional Freemasonry prohibits women from being initiated, and modern Masonry upholds the "boys club" simply for the sake of tradition. Nonetheless, something called Adoptive Masonry exists exclusively for women, while Co-Masonry welcomes all gender identities; these branches, however, are often considered clandestine and have challenging relationships with traditional brotherhoods because they utilize traditional (male) Masonic lessons and initiations rather than independent structures.

Masonry also prohibits the initiation of atheists, with one of the organization's requirements being that members believe in a "supreme being" or higher power. This higher power, however, is up to interpretation. Regardless of Masonry's emphasis on certain Judeo-Christian and biblical allegories within their initiations, the Craft is open to a wide variety of gentlemen who embrace positive spiritual paths.

One of the "old charges" of a Freemason, which goes back as far as 1723, is called *Concerning God and Religion*, and has long been read by many lodges at the Entered Apprentice (first) degree ritual for new brothers of the Craft. This charge asserts that all good men are candidates for Masonry regardless of their religious preference. A section of it reads as follows:

"In ancient Times Masons were charg'd in every Country to be of the Religion of that Country or Nation, whatever it was, yet 'tis now thought more expedient only to oblige them to that Religion in which all Men agree, leaving their particular Opinions to themselves;

that is, to be good Men and true, or Men of Honour and Honesty, by whatever Denominations or Persuasions they may be distinguish'd; whereby Masonry becomes the Center of Union, and the Means of conciliating true Friendship among Persons that must have remain'd at a perpetual Distance."

While most Masons identify with their own country's dominant religion, magicians and Witches of all varieties are members of Masonic lodges. Nothing in Masonry excludes Pagans or occultists. Masonry distinctly celebrates religious diversity and recognizes the forces of honor and honesty as the Center of Union. In theory, Freemasonry's relationship to Witchcraft and the world's multitude of Neopagan religions is no exception. Regardless, Pagans have still had their fair share of struggles with Masonic bodies.

Pagan Problems and Wiccan Worries

Most Masons accept fellow Masons who follow Paganism and occultism, not least because it's considered poor behavior to discuss politics and religion within the confines of a lodge. But not all Pagans have been so lucky.

One recent occasion of anti-Pagan behavior within Masonry occurred in 2012, when the Grand Master of Florida created a particularly divisive statewide edict. Before I describe the occurrence, please allow me to explain what it means to be a Grand Master. Both state and local lodges rotate their various positions on an annual basis. Masonic lodges are their own unique entities but are still under state jurisdiction. A Worshipful Master leads a lodge meeting, while a Grand Master leads state-level gatherings. The Grand Master and his appointed team

uphold and define statewide Masonic protocol and are responsible for organizing statewide gatherings.

In November of 2012, Florida's Grand Master issued a ruling declaring that Wicca, Paganism, Gnosticism, Odinism, and agnosticism are incompatible with Masonic tenets, insisting that Masons can and must *only* believe in the Bible's version of God. It was additionally suggested that brothers identifying under these paths must resign from Masonry altogether—what a dreary prospect! Luckily this declaration was met with global Pagan activism, educational outreach, and a good dose of tongue-in-cheek humor. Masonic Pagans, including myself, would not let go of the issue. Brothers from around the world responded to the edict by writing letters, contacting the media, organizing rallies, writing blogs, and contacting influential Freemasons. In May of 2013, Florida's Grand Lodge overturned the Grand Master's edict while also declaring that religious tolerance is one of the ancient and unchangeable landmarks of the Craft. After all, prejudice is prejudice, regardless of the form it takes.

Personally, I am happy with how the majority of the brothers in my lodge (Missoula Sentinel Lodge #155) have accepted my weirdness. I make no qualms with being a Witch and a Pagan Priest. I'm a fan of nail polish, eyeliner, and wearing an Indian sherwani kurta (fancy tunic) to lodge meetings rather than a suit and tie! I am lucky to be supported by brothers who respect diversity. However, I have encountered other Masons in the state of Montana who have not been so kind, particularly after I arranged a Masonic cover story with a local free newspaper. In the article, the reporters wished to cover our Masonic Temple alongside Freemasonry in general, as well as to explore the individual lives of some of the lodge's younger brothers (our lodge has a relatively high number of younger members).

Because the article examined various brothers' lives, including my own life and the nonprofit Pagan temple I co-operate (called Opus

Aima Obscuræ, or OAO), some of the more conservative Masons in the state raised a fuss, put me under a spotlight, and even suggested putting me on "Masonic trial" because the article explored Witchcraft. They thought this was negative exposure for the Masonic Craft. (The article is called "So Mote It Be" in the *Missoula Independent* and can be looked up online.) Luckily, a number of established members in my own lodge and others came to my defense and averted further prejudice. And while I did not receive thanks for arranging the article—and even though it received controversial reviews by fellow brothers—I am confident that Masonic involvement by liberal and unconventional (yet good-hearted) individuals such as myself and others actually helps the Masonic cause progress and evolve into the twenty-first century.

Magickal Mingling and Crafty Coexistence

It's interesting that some Masons take extreme issue with Pagans, Witches, magicians, and other occultists considering that Masonry has undeniably adopted a plethora of Pagan/occult symbolism and has massively influenced Witches and occultists historically.

Virtually every occult and magickal order in modern times has ties with Freemasonry in some manner. Many notable Freemasons have helped shape modern magick, including Wicca's founder himself, Gerald B. Gardner. Other Freemasons include the illustrious Aleister Crowley, Arthur Edward Waite, Alex Sanders, Eliphas Lévi, William Robert Woodman, Albert Pike, William Wynn Westcott, and Samuel Liddell MacGregor Mathers. And the list goes on!

• • • • • • • • • • • • •

One of Witchcraft's favored affirmations is "So mote it be," often spoken at the end of a ritual, spell, or magickal working. This is an archaic form of "So it shall be." The phrase actually originated in Freemasonry and has been utilized since at least the fifteenth century. During my time as chaplain in my own Masonic lodge, it was my duty to conclude the opening prayers with "Amen," which was followed by all other brothers stating "So mote it be." This is part of the standard Masonic procedure for opening a lodge as a sacred meeting ground and is one of the steps performed for every stated meeting around the world. It is also one of the many little "bridges" between modern Neopagan Witchcraft and the mystical brotherhood of the Freemasons, reminding practitioners that spiritual traditions of all varieties intertwine, intermingle, and can most certainly coexist.

Sources

Greer, John Michael. *Inside a Magical Lodge*. St. Paul, MN: Llewellyn, 1998.

———. *The New Encyclopedia of the Occult*. St. Paul, MN: Llewellyn, 2003.

Hughan, William James. *Constitutions of the Freemasons*. London: R. Spencer, 1869.

Raven Digitalis *(Missoula, MT) is the author of* Esoteric Empathy, Shadow Magick Compendium, Planetary Spells & Rituals, *and* Goth Craft. *He is a Neopagan Priest and cofounder of an "Eastern Hellenistic" nonprofit multicultural temple called Opus Aima Obscuræ (OAO). Also trained in Eastern philosophies and Georgian Witchcraft, Raven has been an earth-based practitioner since 1999, a Priest since 2003, a Freemason since 2012, and an empath all of his life. He holds a degree in anthropology from the University of Montana and is also a professional Tarot reader, DJ, small-scale farmer, and animal rights advocate.*

You can visit Raven online at:
www.ravendigitalis.com
www.facebook.com/ravendigitalis
www.opusaimaobscurae.org
www.facebook.com/opusaimaobscurae

Illustrator: Kathleen Edwards

Embracing Being Broken: How to Avoid Spiritual Bypass

Stephanie Woodfield

I see her shining, the many pieces of herself swirling around her like a whirlwind, like the facets of a diamond. She is serenity and chaos all in one, reminding me that those two forces are more closely linked than I would like to think. She rides atop a crocodile, one foot touching the beast's back, as she navigates the currents of the river that is life, the other foot just slightly raised, balanced in the air as if ready to step off into the heart of the river's currents and its chaos.

This is how I see Akhilandeshvari, the Hindu goddess whose name means

"never not broken." I rather envy her serenity. At times it can be easier to relate to goddesses like Kali, severed heads making up her jewelry and tongue sticking out in rage-filled defiance, or to any of the fierce goddesses who represent strife and overcoming it in some manner. Their fierceness can be easier to understand. But Akhilandeshvari's lessons are necessary before we can embrace the kind of power that fuels Kali.

Akhilandeshvari reminds us that being broken does not mean we are a failure. The moments when we are the most broken are actually our most powerful ones. Yes, when you are a snotty, tear-streaked wreck, doubled over on the floor, you are actually at your most powerful. Why? Because there is nothing holding you back. Our darkest, worst moments can be some of our most defining ones: the moment when we choose change, when we say enough is enough, when we see through the illusions of others or the ones we have held up, when we choose to burn down the framework of our lives and start anew. Very few people just turn around one day and decide to make major changes, needed or not. Sometimes we need a catalyst. We need to fail. We need to be broken, to face our demons and come out the other side knowing they weren't as powerful as we thought they were.

Ironically this isn't a concept we tend to embrace very well. We don't like to fail. We don't like looking at difficult emotions or working through past trauma or even recognizing that our life is falling apart and we really need to do something about it. It's messy, it's painful, and it's not fun. Furthermore, many Pagans shy away from working with gods like Akhilandeshvari who embody the difficult truth of life. She may be at peace with being broken, but most of us have been taught to feel like a failure when we are in such a state.

In general, there is an emphasis on the positive within Paganism. How many times have you heard someone talk about raising their vibration or banishing negativity? We are rather obsessed with getting rid of negativity and finding our Zen to some degree. There is nothing wrong with grounding and centering or blessing one's house or ritual space. I do all of these things. But the danger in concentrating so much on being positive and showing that we have everything together is that then we do not allow ourselves to look at the messy parts of ourselves, or accept that

In general, there is an emphasis on the positive within Paganism. How many times have you heard someone talk about raising their vibration or banishing negativity? We are rather obsessed with getting rid of negativity and finding our Zen to some degree.

we sometimes need those parts. And when this happens, rather than getting closer to a state of enlightenment, we are really sabotaging our spiritual growth.

Not that long ago I attended a workshop on the uses of various crystals and stones. Although the teacher was engaging and I enjoyed the class, by the end of it I realized that more than half of the class had focused on which stones to use to "get rid of" or "banish" negative energy or vibrations. Not only did the teacher talk a great deal about the topic, but most of the attendees had questions that revolved around it. While I stand by the idea that you should never summon something you can't banish, I found myself wondering if we, as Pagans, have a healthy grasp on dealing with the harder parts of life. Because like it or not, being sad and going through difficult times is a natural part of living. After all, where does all the negative energy we are so obsessed with banishing come from?

A spiritual person naturally would look to their spirituality and gods of choice to help them through such challenging times. I certainly have. But more often than not, in Paganism we simply talk about how to get rid of negativity rather than how to really deal with it. We banish it with sage smudge sticks, we see brilliant white light surrounding us, we use stones to negate it, and we are encouraged to be creatures of love and light, to harm ye none. What we don't like to admit is that this approach doesn't always work. You can banish your negativity with a feather and a sage stick all you want, but if you don't actually look at the root of the problem and deal with it—and walk down into your own personal underworlds with the dark gods we often shun in favor of those who teach less difficult lessons—you will never truly banish anything at all. Sometimes our negativity, our anger, our rage, can be useful. Sometimes it's what leads to a breakthrough.

Negativity is an umbrella term that we use to cover everything from anger to the emotional turmoil of a divorce or any other life change. We learn how to smudge, do spells and rituals, and ground and center to combat this ominous "negativity." It's something we are always battling against. We are told never to do magick when we are angry, that the energy would disrupt our magickal goals or not allow us align with our higher self. Yet I've done some pretty powerful work when I was ripping pissed—potent magick that works rather well and quickly, and in which I felt I had justification to be ripping pissed. Some people shrink away from working with dark gods because they think that if they do, bad things will start happening to them. It's not so much that bad things will happen, but rather that dark deities are no-nonsense. If you refuse to face the things they are urging you to look at and conquer, they are pretty good at pinning you in a corner and giving you no other choice.

We like to think that as Pagans we don't have some of the problems other religions have. But we do, and really in many ways we are more susceptible to one in particular. *Spiritual bypass* is a term that was coined in the 1980s by psychotherapist and Buddhist John Welwood, who defined it as the use of spiritual practices or concepts in order to avoid dealing with unresolved emotional or psychological issues. Robert Masters, author of the 2010 book *Spiritual Bypassing*, describes this as "avoidance in holy drag." In his book, Masters says: "We need to stop impaling ourselves on various spiritual shoulds and practices and preoccupations of being nice, positive, and spiritual. We need to recognize and act on addressing our darker or less spiritual emotions, impulses, and intentions and stop denying them as part of who we are. We must be aware of our need to be someone special, spiritual, advanced, and stop dividing everything positive and negative, higher and lower, spiritual and non-spiritual. We want to reach a state of immunity to suffering."[7]

Paganism attracts people for a variety of reasons. Pagan blogger John Halstead proposes that there are four distinct types of Pagans: those who are nature-centered, deity-centered, community-centered, or self-centered.[8] Some Pagans may find that they fall into a single category, while others may fall into more than one camp. There are those whose focus is on nature, seeing the divine in our connection to the earth. The main focus of deity-centered Pagans is their relationship with and worship of the gods, while those centered on their community find fulfillment in maintaining the traditions of what they see as tribe or family.

Self-centered Pagans, according to Halstead's definition, are those who focus on self-improvement, becoming stronger, magically and otherwise, and finding the divine within themselves. And it's this

7. Robert Augustus Masters, *Spiritual Bypassing* (Berkeley, CA: North Atlantic Books), 6.

8. John Halstead, "How 'Gods Before Politics' Perpetuates Privilege," *The Allergic Pagan*, Patheos, July 15, 2016, www.patheos.com/blogs/allergicpagan/2016/07/15/how-gods-before-politics-perpetuates-privilege.

particular group that can be very susceptible to spiritual bypass. The desire to create real and meaningful change in our lives, to cast spells and connect to powerful gods in order to reshape our lives, is a tantalizing thought. We think that if we do just the right spell or say just the right chant, we can land the job of our dreams, find love, and have a happy and content life. Magick *can* do that. But actually manifesting these things isn't as simple as we'd like it to be. What we want is the Emeril Lagasse approach to spiritual growth: BAM! Instant enlightenment and all your problems are dealt with!

But it doesn't work that way. And when we are taught to concentrate so much on being positive and just sweeping our shadow and negative feelings under the rug, we are just prolonging the inevitable. Eventually we will have to deal with those monsters under the bed. And ignoring them just makes it worse.

Spiritual bypass is a trap that anyone can fall into, no matter what religion or spiritual tradition they practice. The trick is to recognize it and not fall into its cycle of avoidance. We need to remember that it's okay to be broken, to be angry, to not have all the answers. You don't have to hurry up and figure your life out. If you do the work, transformation will happen naturally. And it's important that we create safe spaces within our communities and traditions for those dealing with difficult life circumstances and emotions where they can explore transformation and shadow work without stigma.

Spiritual bypass is a trap that anyone can fall into, no matter what religion or spiritual tradition they practice. The trick is to recognize it and not fall into its cycle of avoidance. We need to remember that it's okay to be broken, to be angry, to not have all the answers.

We are not all love and light, perfect love and perfect trust, all the time. Sometimes we have to be like Akhilandeshvari and find power in being broken. And when we are at our worst, when our lives and inner selves are lying shattered on the floor, we are at our most powerful. There are no more illusions; we have embraced our demons. Like Akhilandeshvari, we are broken, and we should celebrate this. It means we get to pick up the pieces and decide what the new shape of ourselves can be. And being positive, always seeing the good things, won't get us there. Sometimes the greatest wisdom can be gained only through pain and tears.

Invocation to Akhilandeshvari

Akhilandeshvari,
Never-Not-Broken,
I call to you.
Lady who is constantly in motion,
You who tear apart yourself
Again and again,
Ever changing, every recreating yourself,
May I navigate the currents of life
Knowing there is beauty in change,
Beauty in being broken.

Resources

Beckett, John. "The Four Centers of Paganism." Patheos, May 28, 2014. www.patheos.com/blogs/johnbeckett/2014/05/the-four-centers-of-paganism.html.

Fossella, Tina. "Human Nature, Buddha Nature: On Spiritual Bypassing, Relationship, and the Dharma: An Interview with John Welwood." *Tricycle* (Spring 2011). Available at www.johnwelwood.com/articles/TRIC_interview_uncut.pdf.

Masters, Robert Augustus, PhD. *Spiritual Bypassing*. Berkeley, CA: North Atlantic Books, 2010.

Stephanie Woodfield *is the author of* Celtic Lore & Spellcraft of the Dark Goddess: Invoking the Morrigan *and* Drawing Down the Sun: Rekindle the Magick of the Solar Goddesses. *Stephanie has been a practicing Witch and Priestess of the Morrigan for over sixteen years. Her articles have appeared in* SageWoman *magazine and* The Portal *and on the* Witches' Voice *website. She is one of the founding members of* Morrigu's Daughters, *an online sisterhood dedicated to the Morrigan. Visit her blog,* Dark Goddess Musings, *at http://darkgoddessmusings.blogspot.com.*

Illustrator: Tim Foley

Creatures of an Elder World: In Pursuit of Shakespeare's Three Witches

Linda Raedisch

A few Christmases ago, when my older daughter gave my younger daughter a copy of *Doctor Who: The Visual Dictionary (Updated and Expanded)*, she stuck Post-It notes over all the alien faces she feared might give her little sister nightmares. Those notes have since been removed, but I'm all for slapping them back on the ghastly mugs of the Carrionites. The Carrionites, for those of you unacquainted with the Whoniverse, are a malevolent race from the Rexel planetary system. They ride on broomsticks and work magic through the use of cantrips, poppets, and scrying bowls. And *man* are they ugly!

When three especially nasty Carrionites attempt to use the Globe Theatre as a platform for world domination, it is, of course, up to the Doctor to stop them. This all happened back in 1599, time enough for the Carrionites to inspire Shakespeare to create the characters of the Three Witches in *Macbeth*.

But let's get real. In the first folio of *Macbeth*, Shakespeare doesn't call these characters "Witches" at all, but "weyard women." *Weyard*, in modern spelling, is *weird*, a word we'll examine more closely later. Shakespeare did not invent the otherworldly creatures who nudged the Thane of Glamis to his doom; he borrowed them from historical writers who had drafted them from older chronicles still and ultimately from oral tradition.

When Macbeth and Banquo first encounter them on the moors, the Weird Sisters appear in their primordial forms, looking more like features of the landscape than mortal women. When Banquo says, "What are these / So withered and so wild in their attire, / That look not like th' inhabitants o' th' earth, / And yet are on't?" we can be sure his hair is standing on end. These creatures appear not to belong to the world of men. Banquo is surprised when they "seem to understand" him, while Macbeth commands them, "Speak if you can," as if they might not be capable of human speech.

If you want to meet up with Macbeth's Witches today, you might want to start looking in the neighborhood of the Moray Firth, specifically in the town of Forres, inside the glass case housing a late Pictish monument known as Sueno's Stone. Sueno's Stone commemorates the victory of one early Scottish king over another—not, however, Malcolm's victory over Macbeth, for the stone was already old in their time. According to one story, the Weird Sisters are imprisoned here, drawn inside the stone like genies into a lamp or like Carrionites into the crystal ball in which the Doctor eventually trapped them ("Spoilers!").

If you want to meet up with Macbeth's Witches today, you might want to start looking in the neighborhood of the Moray Firth, specifically in the town of Forres, inside the glass case housing a late Pictish monument known as Sueno's Stone.

Another logical place to look is the nearby Macbeth's Hillock where the Thane of Glamis is supposed to have first clapped eyes on the women who would tell him his destiny. Rippling with purple heather, thistles, and heavy-headed grasses, the Hillock is hardly the bleak and "blasted" heath that Shakespeare makes it out to be. Did the Weird Sisters ever actually appear here?

In his *Hierarchie of the Blessed Angels*, Thomas Heywood (a contemporary of Shakespeare) has "Mackbeth and Banco-Stuart" riding along "in a darke Grove" on that fateful day. And Raphael Holinshed's *Chronicles* (1577), of which Shakespeare certainly owned a copy, has the two men "passing through wodes and fieldes" where they behold "iii women in straunge and ferly apparel, resembling creatures of an elder worlde." Scotland was a lot woodsier prior to the mid-1800s when many of its forests, like Birnam Wood, were cleared away, but Shakespeare must have felt that a barren heath better foreshadowed the doom that was to befall Macbeth.

In the cast of characters in later folios of *Macbeth*, Shakespeare introduces the ladies as "Three Witches, the Weird Sisters," to distinguish them, one supposes, from ordinary Witches. They had never before been identified as such but as "three Virgins wondrous faire" (Heywood) and "the weird sisters…the Goddesses of Destinie, or else some Nimphes or Feiries" (Holinshed). The closest Holinshed comes to calling them Witches is to suggest that they might be "endewed with knowledge of prophecie by their necromanticall science."

So why did Shakespeare sketch such a frightful portrait of [the Weird Sisters] in *Macbeth*? The answer lies with Shakespeare's patron, King James I, newly arrived from Scotland and one of the most Witchophobic monarchs in history.

They certainly don't *look* like Witches in the woodcut accompanying the account in the *Chronicles*. Dressed to the nines in puffed sleeves, surcoats, and brocade skirts, they're fashionable women of the times. So why did Shakespeare sketch such a frightful portrait of them in *Macbeth*?

The answer lies with Shakespeare's patron, King James I, newly arrived from Scotland and one of the most Witchophobic monarchs in history. You can't really blame James; horror stories concerning Witches had been circulating within the Scottish royal house long before Macbeth picked up a dagger. In 968, a company of Forres Witches were executed for roasting a waxen image of King Duffus as well as attempting to poison him. In 1537, the beautiful Janet Douglas, Lady Glamis, was accused of using her deadly charms against James V of Scotland. The king survived, but Janet, whom many believed to be innocent, was burned at the stake.

And then, in 1590, John Fian, aka the "Devil's secretary," allegedly conjured a storm to sink a ship carrying James VI (later James I of England) and his Danish bride. Though the assassination attempt failed, John Fian was tortured and burned along with a handful of his North Berwick coven. Considering this family history of Witch burning, along with his own personal experience, James may even have felt that Shakespeare had not laid the loathliness on thickly enough. Sure, the Three Witches are ugly, but they never actually plot against the king; they only prophesy.

The Weird Sisters' number is the one thing Shakespeare, Heywood, Holinshed, and Andrew of Wyntoun, scribbling his own version of events in the early fifteenth century, can agree on. In Scotland, as elsewhere in the Jacobean world, thirteen was the norm for coven membership. Unearthly women who appear consistently in threes are necessarily of older stock. Heywood calls them simply "Virgins" and "Maids," but Wyntoun and Holinshed both include the term "weird sisters." *Weird* is a loaded word, coming from the Old English *wyrd*, meaning "fate." Weirdness, then, did not denote strangeness, though Holinshed's women do, in fact, appear "straunge"—that is, they cause one to wonder, to be astonished. (Holinshed's "ferly" means just about the same as Heywood's "wondrous.") Yes, these women are beautiful, but it is such a strange sort of beauty that you have to wonder if it is real.

The Weird Sisters, then, are no ordinary Witches but are the embodiment of wyrd, the whole of one's past, present, and future.

The Norsemen called them *Norns*, and while the sagas mention many Norns—so many that at times "Norn" seems to be an ethnic identity or a member of an international secret society—the three most important are Urd, Verdandi, and Skuld, whose names can be translated as "becoming," "being," and "that which will be." The noun *wyrd* comes from *weorthan*, "to become," which has the secondary meaning of "to turn." The Norns, like most women of the Bronze, Iron, and Middle Ages, spent much of their time twirling their spindles. The Norns spin the threads of destiny, snipping them off when our numbers are up.

The Norns, like most women of the Bronze, Iron, and Middle Ages, spent much of their time twirling their spindles. The Norns spin the threads of destiny, snipping them off when our numbers are up.

By Macbeth's time, the Vikings, along with their reverence for the Norns, had been ensconced in Orkney and the Outer Hebrides for over a hundred years. Old Sueno, or "Sven," whose name became associated with the stone at Forres, was also a Norseman. As the eleventh century progressed, the Scots (already an amalgam of immigrant Gaels and native Picts) would be running into these Germanic settlers more and more often, no longer just on the battlefield but also at weddings and christenings.

Imagine yourself as a loyal subject of the Kingdom of Alba (northern Scotland) and a member of either the Celtic or the Pictish Church, as your family has been for generations. You've been invited to a christening—a "name fastening," they call it—by one of your Nordic

neighbors. Seated in the richly decorated hall, you're slightly repulsed by the Pagan atmosphere prevailing at the feast. The jarl is at least a nominal Christian, but old traditions die hard. As you dip your bannock in the broth, careful to avoid the chunks of horsemeat floating in it, you notice three old ladies hovering over the cradle on the dais. They're being treated as honored guests despite their dirty shawls, the plainness of their brooches, and the fact that they have brought no gift for the child except a bunch of leeks.

In fact, they *have* brought gifts, just not ones that you can see. These homely women are spaewives, mortal representatives of the Norns, born with the gift of second sight, come to tell the newborn's fortune. After they have spoken their part, they retire to a corner of the hall to enjoy their meal, share the gossip of the countryside, and, no doubt, get a little spinning done.

The Norns belong to the Germanic cosmos, but such spirits are, in fact, a broader Indo-European phenomenon. They have been with us since the invention of the drop spindle. Like the Norns, the Greek Fates occupied themselves with the spinning, measuring, and cutting of the threads of destiny. The Scandinavian Urd, whose name is an Old Norse cognate of the Old English *Wyrd*, was sometimes identified as the oldest of the Norns and may once have been a singular goddess of fate. Skuld was said to be the youngest of the Norns, which would suggest that at one time there were only two. And indeed, the Hittites, whose language was one of the first to branch off from the trunk of the Indo-European language tree, recognized only two spinning goddesses of the underworld: Istustaya and Papaya. These ladies could be found busily twirling their spindles on a Black Sea beach. They also possessed "filled mirrors," which were probably vessels of

water in which they descried the future—precursors, perhaps, of the mirror in which Shakespeare's Macbeth observed the succession of Banquo's sons.

The purpose of spinning is to make thread for weaving into cloth: mantles, bed curtains, banners, and the brightly embroidered pennants that warriors tied to the shafts of their spears. Battles were a favorite subject of tapestries, from the rich hangings in a Viking jarl's hall to the Bayeux "Tapestry" (actually crewelwork on a plain linen ground) commemorating William of Normandy's conquest of England in 1066. In the *Saga of Helgi Hundingsbane*, the Norns presiding over Helgi's birth weave an immense tapestry depicting the hero's destiny. And in *Njal's Saga*, twelve Valkyries, close cousins of the Norns, weave the outcome of the Battle of Clontarf, before it's fought, on a bloody warp of men's intestines.

Like the saga writers who recounted these dreamlike episodes, Andrew of Wyntoun tells us that Macbeth met the Weird Sisters not in real time but "in his dremynge." In the dream, Macbeth is out hunting in the forest with his greyhounds when he meets three women in passing. This sounds very much like an adventure of the legendary Høther in *The History of the Danes*, an amalgam of history and myth compiled in the early thirteenth century. Høther, too, is out on the hunt when he runs into some "forest maidens" idling outside their house. They greet Høther by name, even though he has never seen them before, and explain to him how they haunt the fields of battle, awarding success to those they favor and defeat to those they do not. They offer Høther a piece of advice concerning his rivalry with the demigod Balder and then they vanish, just as Holinshed's women do, leaving "Makbeth and Banquho" to suppose it had been "some vayne fantasticall illusion."

Høther meets the women while awake, but then, Høther's whole life is like a dream. He has a magic sword and an impenetrable coat of mail. Gods wander in and out of his adventures. Had Macbeth never acted upon his vision of the Weird Sisters, maybe that's all it would have been: a dream.[9] The Norns spin, measure, and cut the threads of our lives, but it's up to us to dye them.

The Three Witches' true abode is not anywhere in Scotland (or in the Rexel planetary system) but in the shade of Yggdrasil, the ancient ash tree whose three roots are planted in the sacred white mud of the underworld. Its trunk rises up, spindle-straight, through the Nine Worlds of the Norse cosmos, of which our world, Manheim, is the fifth. Where in Manheim you happen to meet the Three Witches is wherever you meet your destiny.

While I was in the home stretch of this article's first draft, I suddenly realized that, in a way, the Weird Sisters had been a fixture of my childhood. I had three "aunts" who did everything together, so much so that we had a collective name for them: the "West Orangers," after the old house they shared on a leafy street in West Orange, New Jersey. (The name stuck even after they moved to Lakewood.) Their house was crammed with porcelain dolls, grandfather clocks, Austrian beeswax sculptures, and other mementos of a lifetime spent traveling together. The West Orangers weren't sisters, and none of them actually spun, but they were never without their knitting. One of them was my godmother, so all three attended my birthday parties, bulging bags of yarn in tow. Aunt Dot, a widow, was the oldest by a decade or more. She would be Urd. Aunt Ellen, a "spinster," was the youngest by only a few weeks, but she was far and away the most girlish of the three. She would be Skuld. That left my godmother, the divorcée Aunt Fran, to fill the role of Verdandi.

Aunt Fran liked to give me books for Christmas and birthdays, a tradition our family carries on to this day. While planning my own

---

9. The Norns spun a very different lifespan for the real Macbeth, who came by his throne fair and square and died in battle at Lumphanan after a long and more or less peaceful reign.

book, *The Old Magic of Christmas*, I turned repeatedly to the "Christmas around the World" books she had ordered for me over the years. Could she have guessed that I was going to be a writer, specifically a chronicler of obscure traditions? All three of the West Orangers are gone now, so all I can do is wonder who might get *this* book for a Christmas or birthday present and where it might take them.

Sources Not Mentioned in the Text

Aitchison, Nick. *Macbeth: Man and Myth*. Gloucester, England: Sutton Publishing, 2000.

Briggs, K. M. *Pale Hecate's Team: An Examination of the Beliefs on Witchcraft and Magic among Shakespeare's Contemporaries and His Immediate Successors*. New York: The Humanities Press, 1962.

Bryce, Trevor. *Life and Society in the Hittite World*. Oxford: Oxford University Press, 2002.

Taylor, Cameron, and Alistair Murray. *On the Trail of the Real Macbeth, King of Alba*. Edinburgh: Luath Press, 2008.

Linda Raedisch *makes a point of looking for the otherworldly in the everyday. To date, she has written two books for Llewellyn and more articles than she can easily count. Though the walls of her home are now lined with reference books, including the fateful "Christmas around the World" series, she's just as likely to find inspiration in an episode of* Doctor Who *or by gazing into the depths of a strong cup of tea.*

Illustrator: Jennifer Hewitson

How to Start a Pagan Blog

Elizabeth Barrette

Blogging is a fun and effective way to reach out to people and share your ideas. You can write about anything and post it online. What you write depends on your purpose for starting a blog. It may be for education, community connection, personal expression, or other reasons. Pagans in particular find blogging helpful for interacting with others in their faith, especially if there aren't enough people locally to form a coven.

A blog also allows you to share developing observations over time. As your experiences change, so will your posts. You

can then look back over earlier ones to see how things have evolved. This is valuable if you have just begun studying Paganism, if you teach students about your faith, or if your coven holds regular events that you want to promote and remember.

It is easier and more efficient to begin blogging when you do some planning first. Let's look at some helpful steps.

Choosing a Topic

The topic for your blog can be as wide or narrow as you want. Some people just write about whatever catches their fancy that day. Within the context of this discussion, a Pagan blog is necessarily topical. You may want to write about one specific thing that changes over time, such as the Wheel of the Year, or about a handful of related subtopics, such as exploring the deities from different pantheons. The narrower the topic, the deeper you can go with it. The broader the topic, the more ground you can cover. It depends on your taste.

There are all kinds of ways to choose a focus for your blog. If something already fascinates you, then by all means write about it. If you don't have a specific subject yet, then look at various Pagan blogs already in print and try to find either a new topic or a new angle on a current topic so that you're not duplicating other people's efforts. Understand that it is much easier to stand out from the crowd if you write about something uncommon, but conversely, many more people will set out searching for the popular topics. So it's a tradeoff. Let's consider some possible subjects.

Your Personal Path

Many people blog about their discovery of Paganism and what they have learned. Each journey is unique in its own way.

The Gods

You can write about one deity (such as Cernunnos), a particular class (such as moon goddesses), or a pantheon (such as Hawaiian), or you can ramble among different ones.

Spellcraft

Magic is very popular, and people often search for spells to cast. Whether you write about the theory or the practice, this can attract a lot of readers. You may wish to rotate through different types, such as spells for love, prosperity, healing, etc.

Specialties

Most Pagans have one or more skills. You could write about divination, astrology, stone magic, energy work, herbalism, and so forth.

Coven or Solitary Work

Group dynamics can provide endless inspiration, whereas private practice offers opportunities for introspection. Since everyone is either working together or working alone, you have an audience with either focus.

Choosing a Venue

There are two basic options for hosting a blog. One is to put it on your own website, and the other is to use a blogging service. Compare and contrast the features of possible hosts before selecting one. Using your own website requires more skill to build the site in the first place, more money if you pay for hosting, and more work to attract an audience. However, you get much more control over what you can do with it. A blogging service's big advantages are the large pool of users and the ease of construction, plus most of them are free at the basic level, although some offer premium features for a fee. The downside is that they're more likely to set restrictions, and they may kick you off for any reason or no reason. For Pagans, this is really important.

The most vital step in choosing a host for your Pagan blog is to make sure that it is either Pagan-friendly or tolerant of diversity. In theory, America guarantees religious freedom, but in practice, Pagans get stepped on plenty. Look for a host that already has some other Pagan blogs, if possible, or at least has a wide variety of religions represented. Such hosts are less likely to hassle you about your topic, and you don't

The most vital step in choosing a host for your Pagan blog is to make sure that it is either Pagan-friendly or tolerant of diversity.

WP
W
D
VENUE ST.

want to do all the work of launching a blog just to have someone delete it because they dislike your religion. For this reason, it is also advisable to back up your content on your own hard drive.

WordPress

This tool is a complex, relatively powerful way to create your own website or blog for free. You need to understand some coding to make it work, but you can do a lot with it.

LiveJournal

This is one of the older blogging networks. It's a bit buggy, but it offers easy-to-use templates, generous post size, and a substantial audience.

Dreamwidth

This service is among the newer blogging networks. It's still in active development, with a modest but growing audience and nice templates. Dreamwidth one is getting better over time.

Designing a Layout

The layout of your blog influences its effectiveness. People typically read a page in one of two patterns: F or Z. In both cases, the most attention falls on the upper left corner, so put your most important information there. The top line gets moderate traffic, followed by the lower left corner. Lighter attention goes to the middle (F) or the lower right (Z). People should know you have a Pagan blog immediately, so try to incorporate that into your title bar or left corner logo. Put less urgent material farther down.

Choose colors with an eye toward legibility first and magical correspondences second. People can't read what they can't see clearly. That means you need something with high contrast and low irritation. Black on white and white on black both work well, although bright white can cause eyestrain after a while. Soft colors work great as long as you maintain contrast. I like black print on very pale blue for my blogs, with darker blues for framing. Avoid very bright colors in large blocks. Yes, some people have a bold red background, but that doesn't make it a good idea.

How do you use brighter colors? They work well for titles, subtitles, and link text—small things you want to emphasize so people can find them. Images serve a similar purpose and also help break up the text. In a blog, this is often accomplished with post frames and user avatars, but you can also insert images into your posts. This is where you should consider magical correspondences, such as your patron deity's colors or a green/brown palette for earth magic. If you use a blogging host, look closely at the offered templates, because many of them actually have elemental or other magical references. Pagans do code!

Avoid things that annoy people. Don't put ads all over your site. If you must have some, put them on the bottom and make sure they are relevant to your content. Anything that blinks or moves is especially bad, because it distracts people from your writing. Don't set music, videos, or any other sound to play automatically; use a button so people who want those things can turn the features on and off. Use an accessibility monitor to measure how well your site meets special needs. It will tell you if your contrast is good, your graphics have appropriate text tags, and so forth. Good accessibility maximizes your potential audience.

Posting Content

The most important part of a blog is the content. You must write interesting material in order to attract an audience. Frequency and reliability are two key aspects of this. Blogs that update more often become popular faster than those that do so less often, to a certain point. Too much traffic can overwhelm readers. Updating once a day to several times a day is ideal. You need to post at least once a week for best effect. If you can't post every day, make a schedule—such as Monday, Wednesday, Friday—and stick to it.

Consider three basic types of posts. **Anchor posts** are long, original discussions of a topic. You need periodic anchor posts to show your knowledge of the blog's subject area, ideally with things your readers can't easily find elsewhere. **Recurring posts** are questions you revisit regularly, such as a Friday reprise of your weekly activities or a monthly esbat report. These build continuity, especially if you ask your readers what they are doing too. **Forwards** include all manner of things written by other people that pertain to your topic, whether you're forwarding posts within a blogging network or linking to outside news articles. For best effect, include your own opinions about the material rather than just pointing to it. Forwards that include your

own commentary add variety and also keep your blog active without requiring you to write everything yourself.

In a Pagan blog, look for interesting bits of your main topic that you haven't seen other people writing about, or where you disagree with the current materials, and make those your anchor posts. Esbats, sabbats, and other seasonal stuff make good recurring posts. Look for news about Pagan issues, because that's not always easy to find—you can attract an audience just by serving as a really good newsfeed for people.

Building an Audience

Half of a blog is the writer, and the other half is the audience. When you write, you communicate not just about your subject but also about yourself. Readers today like to get to know their writers. So blogging is also a great way to make friends.

First, introduce yourself to your readers. Tell them who you are and how you got here. Explain why you want to write a Pagan blog, and share some of the important things happening in your life right now. You don't have to reveal personal information—indeed, be cautious about doing that online—but make sure readers understand your credentials for writing about this stuff.

Next, establish expectations. Cyberspace is a lot like Underhill in fairy tales: it is what you make of it. You get what you permit and what you reward. So if you expect people to behave decently and you remove those who misbehave, you build up a nice place. It is easier for people to meet your expectations when they know what those are. Therefore, begin with clear ground rules about what you will be doing (such as your topic and posting schedule) and what you want them to do (such as be polite). Set boundaries for things you will not allow, and enforce those. To do this, you need strong moderation tools; you can do what you want on your own site, and a good blogging network should allow you to suspend or ban trolls. Understand that if you don't moderate your blog, it is likely to turn into a brawl fairly often; if you manage it responsibly, you will attract positive people who will help you keep it running smoothly.

A good blogging network should allow you to suspend or ban trolls. Understand that if you don't moderate your blog, it is likely to turn into a brawl fairly often; if you manage it responsibly, you will attract positive people who will help you keep it running smoothly.

Finally, use audience interaction to attract and keep good readers. If you're hosting your own blog, you'll have to do some extra work to build an audience using ads or other methods. Handing out flyers or business cards at a Pagan event may also help. Blogging networks often have an invite feature, or you can look for blogs you like and comment there until people follow you back to yours. In your posts, ask questions that get people talking. Pay attention to your regular commenters and respond to their input. Answer comments as often as you can. Once you have a month or so of posts, ask readers what they'd like to see more or less of. Let them help you develop your blog. They'll come up with ideas you never would have thought of on your own.

Writing a Pagan blog can be a great adventure. Following the steps for advance planning will improve your chances of success. Think about what you want to write, find an appropriate host, set up your blog, and start writing. Adapt as you go along. Usually you can build up a useful amount of audience interaction within a few weeks, but it takes about a year to establish a blog—or most new projects—securely enough to last over the long term. So plan ahead and good luck!

Elizabeth Barrette *has been involved with the Pagan community for more than twenty-seven years. She served as managing editor of* PanGaia *for eight years and dean of studies at the Grey School of Wizardry for four years. She has written columns on beginning and intermediate Pagan practice, Pagan culture, and Pagan leadership. Her book* Composing Magic: How to Create Magical Spells, Rituals, Blessings, Chants, and Prayers *explains how to combine writing and spirituality. She lives in central Illinois, where she has done much networking with Pagans in her area, such as coffeehouse meetings and open sabbats. Her other public activities feature Pagan picnics and science fiction conventions. She enjoys magical crafts, historical religions, and gardening for wildlife. Her other writing fields include speculative fiction, gender studies, social and environmental issues. Visit her blog,* The Wordsmith's Forge *(http://ysabetwordsmith.livejournal.com) or her website,* PenUltimate Productions *(http://penultimateproductions.weebly.com). Her coven site, which includes extensive Pagan materials, is* Greenhaven Tradition *(http://greenhaventradition.weebly.com).*

Illustrator: Rik Olson

Witchy Living

Day-by-Day Witchcraft

Everyday Witchcraft

Jason Mankey

It's hard to be an everyday Witch. The stresses of work and family, not to mention the constant distractions of social media, cellphones, and TV, often get in the way of the Craft. In the crazy 24/7 environment most of us live in, it's easy to go days or even weeks at a time without practicing any sort of Witchcraft. Most of us don't have time to ritualize on a daily basis, but there are lots of little things we can do every day to bring us closer to the Lord and Lady and grow our inner Witch.

My personal practice of Witchcraft generally revolves around three primary

concerns: deity (the Lord and Lady), the natural world, and magick. I don't celebrate all three aspects on a daily basis, but I do take at least a few minutes each day to honor one of them. Everyday practice doesn't have to be all-encompassing and time-consuming; it's simply a way to honor the powers that shape our lives and bring us closer to the mysteries of the Craft.

Devotions to Deity

I became a Wiccan-Witch because of the Lord and Lady. They are more than just deities; they are entities that provide me with guidance and reassurance during difficult times. In my own practice, I honor particular goddesses and gods (Pan, Brigit, etc.) and the more general Goddess and God. I acknowledge particular aspects of the divine depending on whatever circumstances I find myself in. If my marriage is going particularly well, I might honor Aphrodite, and if I feel disconnected from the natural world, I call to the Gaulish-Celtic Cernunnos.

The easiest way to get in contact with the Lord and Lady is simply to talk to them, and I find that I'm never too busy to say a few words to deity. Where we speak to them doesn't matter either. Sometimes they are easier to get in touch with outdoors or at an indoor altar, but if you've built a good relationship with deity over the years, your gods are never far away. *Prayer* is often a dirty word in Witch circles, but praying to deity and talking with them are essentially the same thing.

I do not believe that my gods demand sacrifice, but it pleases me on a personal level to present them with offerings. In a ritual context, such offerings are often called *libations*. The most common offerings are food and drink, things we touch and consume every day. Most mornings I check on the garden in my backyard and often share a little bit of my coffee with the gods while doing so. Before pouring my morning eye-opener on the ground, I usually say a few words to whatever deity I'm leaving it for. When no particular deity catches my fancy in the morning, I sometimes just say, "To the earth."

While an offering of coffee works quite well as a morning libation, my favorite gift to leave for the gods is alcohol. Most of them seem to really appreciate a fine wine, and many of my favorite Celtic deities enjoy quality scotch. A proper offering is one that means something to you; it's not an excuse to get rid of things you don't like.

In addition to sharing with the Lord and Lady, I also occasionally leave gifts in my backyard to the fey (fairy folk) who live there. They seem to like shiny things, and I've left them jewelry, glass beads, and small clay offerings over the years. While I don't feel like I have to placate deity with material things, I think it's a good idea to do so with the fey. I want to remain on their good side.

Connecting to the Earth and the Natural World

The eight great Wiccan sabbats are essentially holidays that honor the earth. We celebrate the natural world on those days and honor its rhythms, gifts, and promises. Simply decorating for autumn with tiny gourds and pumpkins can connect us to the earth's cycles in a very meaningful way. Even easier is to just walk outside and find something worth appreciating. It could be something alive and growing, like a tree, or a feature of the world around you, such as a blue sky, a mountain, or the morning dew.

As a Witch, I honor the natural world by respecting the powers of the four basic elements: earth, air, fire, and water. At the altar in my office I often take a moment each day to acknowledge their presence in my life. This might be something as simple as lighting a stick of incense for air and fire, or mixing up a solution of salt and water and

sprinkling it around my workspace to rid it of negativity. What's most important to me in such operations is simply acknowledging the elements and visualizing my connection to the earth through them.

Not everyone has the space, time, and green thumb necessary to plant a garden (or even to tend a solitary potted plant), but there are few better ways to connect to the natural world on a daily basis. Keeping the fruit trees in my backyard alive is a matter of personal pride and is a great daily way to remain in contact with the earth. At times when I'm unable to garden, just going to my local farmers' market on a regular basis keeps me plugged in to the bounties the earth has to offer in my location.

Service to the earth is another way to grow one's Witchcraft. There are formal things we can do as Witches to help our world, such as adopting a local highway or participating in recycling efforts, but there are small things we can do, too. Just picking up some trash while out on a walk or properly recycling electronic waste can help make the world a little brighter—and a little cleaner.

A Magickal Path

Wiccan-Witchcraft is a magickal religion, and magick is an essential part of what we do as Witches. Magick isn't just a way to change and influence our circumstances; it's how we commune with the gods and honor the earth. Magickal workings are essential to the practice of any well-rounded Witch.

When we think of magick, we tend to imagine complicated spells with lots of ingredients and other accoutrements. Those things are helpful, of course, but they aren't necessary. The most basic form of magick is creative visualization, which involves picturing what you want (or are trying to do) in your mind's eye and then releasing that intention out into the universe. This is a technique I use when tedious tasks start to get frustrating or I'm simply not doing the things

I should do (like write or exercise). It's also a good way to center and focus when you find yourself going astray.

As a Witch, I have many magickal tools, and taking a few minutes here and there to clean and polish them is another way to build a daily practice. Touching and working with our tools, even if it's just wiping down an athame with a cloth, imparts a bit of personal energy to our magickal implements. This will make them more effective in both spellwork and ritual.

Many Witches see spells as one-off affairs, but many of my most effective spells have been cast over days or even weeks. Working the same spell over an extended period of time adds extra focus and intent to the working. A long-gestating spell is a daily reminder of just how powerful and transformative Witchcraft can be. Tapping into the magickal current of the universe can also be refreshing and empowering.

. . . .

Witchcraft isn't limited to full moons and sabbat rites; it's a way of life. Building an effective personal Craft requires a dash of magick and devotion on a daily basis. By practicing a little something each and every day, we grow closer to the earth and the Lord and Lady—which makes us better Witches.

Jason Mankey *is a Wiccan-Witch, writer, and wannabe rock and roller. He has been part of the greater Pagan community for over twenty years and has spent nearly half that time teaching and speaking at Pagan conventions across the United States and Canada. He has written two books for Llewellyn,* The Witch's Athame *(2016) and* The Witch's Book of Shadows *(2017), and is also the channel manager of* Patheos Pagan *online. He lives in Sunnyvale, California, where he and his wife, Ari, help lead two local covens. Because they don't want to be outnumbered, Ari and Jason have only two cats.*

Illustrator: Kathleen Edwards

Hardware Store Magick

Diana Rajchel

There are few things as gratifying to a Witch with a project as an occult shop. The books that you drool over, the wafting incense, the shine of the crystals, the fascinating knickknacks and herbs to delight any Witch's inner magpie ... Nothing will ever replace the blessed shop. Yet for the determined magician, any place can be an occult supplier if you have the know-how, attention, and imagination. Dollar stores, craft stores, city sidewalks, bowling alleys, coffee shops—they all have potential for the Witch on a mission. But today—today is all about the hardware store.

Most Witches have found themselves in this situation at some point: You're short on time because you have three errands to run, two of which place you across town from your preferred botanica half an hour before it closes. You could run across town for that charm you need, but that would leave you with very little breathing room. Better to look for supplies where you are: near a big box hardware store. Walk in and acknowledge that sea of drill bits and mysterious items called Craftsman. What you really see, on the crowded shelves of seemingly random objects, is an ocean of infinite possibilities. The first tool of Witchcraft is imagination—and yes, you can bring it with you to Home Depot.

Your purposes may vary: love or money, a bug trap for a pesky, untranquil spirit, or maybe something to bring fairies to your garden.

The following are just a few of the many, many things a hardware store has to offer a Witch.

Screws and Nails

While coffin nails hold a special place in the hearts of Hoodoo practitioners, and rusty nails are preferred for the ever-useful Witch bottle, they aren't required. Nails can rust just fine after you put them in the bottle, and coffin nails are just nails that happened to be used in or intended for a coffin. The magical use of nails and screws can extend to all sorts of workings: nails also come in handy when etching symbols on a candle or into clay (did you know you can make your own clay?), and the iron makes them an effective protection charm against evil, especially when you shape two of them into a cross and bind them together with twine or wire.

Screws, while able to do most of what a nail can, have added symbolism due to their spiral shape, their use as a means of facilitating movement between joints, and their ability to hold heavy objects in place longer than a nail might. You can use the spiral of a screw to imbue the land around a property with a specific emotional state, "pressing" a sense of peace or vitality into the land itself. You can even use the screw to "infect" the walls it touches with that specific mood, as you drive the spiral in and imagine the mood spreading throughout your home. The twisting action may also "twist" negative intentions sent your way, warping them into something that serves your highest good.

Mirrors

If you have watched any iteration of *Snow White and the Seven Dwarfs*, you are familiar with magic mirrors. While they are the most popular (and affordable) tool for scrying, they also offer a host of other possibilities as sources of reflection and manifestation. While a mirror is often used as either a divination tool or a means of defense, its place in manifestation work cannot be ignored. Painting a sigil or doing an image transfer of what you want onto a surface can act as a psychic 3-D printer.

You need not limit yourself to actual mirrors; any reflective surface bears the metaphysical qualities of a mirror. Hardware stores sell hoards of such items, including tape, metal pipes, wires, and metal sheeting. Adapt the intention of the mirror to the shape of its surface. For example, a round mirror might serve as a shield that bounces back negative energy. A reflective surface in narrow form, such as a metal tube or pipe, might represent a work pipeline, and a path you wish to reverse or change.

Tile

Many chain hardware stores have free tile sample displays so customers can take a piece home and compare it with fabric swatches and paint samples. A single ceramic tile comes in handy for use as a heatproof stand for a small cast-iron cauldron, as a place for charcoal incense, or as the spot on which to rest a pillar candle burning for a specific purpose. Some practitioners might paint a sigil on one of these tiles and use it for daily meditation until a goal is accomplished. Ceremonial magic workers can arrange tiles into flashing colors for shifting consciousness and color energy workings.

A single ceramic tile comes in handy for use as a heatproof stand for a small cast-iron cauldron, as a place for charcoal incense, or as the spot on which to rest a pillar candle burning for a specific purpose.

Houseplants and Seeds

Most hardware stores also have a garden section. Since plants form the roots of most Witchcraft practices, even the mechanically disinclined may venture into hardware stores for these offerings. Witch-friendly plants that are common in hardware stores include ferns, date palms, and ivy. While we often associate these plants with office spaces seeking a barrier against the existential dread induced by fluorescent lighting and gray-brown cubicle walls, they also act as fabulous air filters. Each plant also has an association/purpose related to Witchcraft. Ferns ward off trouble; their seeds are used to promote invisibility and have powerful associations with Midsummer/St. John's Eve. Ivy has a long tradition as a protective plant, both inside and outside the home. Date palms are especially potent; not only can they enhance male sexuality, but the leaves also drive off astral nasties.

Most hardware stores carry seeds on a seasonal basis, and almost any plant is popular among the witchy set. Basil, fennel, tomato, hyssop, and rosemary are often among the standard seed packets available, all of which have rich herbal folklore behind them. While most people buy seeds with the intention to plant them, the seeds themselves are useful in potions and incenses, especially those intended to release potential.

Soil

Those with the funds to travel may enjoy collecting different types of soil from around the world for different purposes. Sometimes, however, you need to bury a poppet, you have no car, and that strip of trees at the edge of the mall parking lot always has a security vehicle right there. On those occasions, just use potting soil. You can bury that poppet, put your energetically buzzing ritual jewelry into a flowerpot to ground, or use a soil-filled flowerpot as a spot to cool your cauldron—a peat-based soil is best for this last purpose.

Grow Lights

Most people think of grow lights as fancy tables and tubes meant to hover over gigantic trays of plants, usually of dubious legality. Yet grow lights come in forms much more affordable than those used by gardeners dedicated to growing exotic crops. A simple grow bulb costs less than ten dollars and can fit in a basic desk lamp. A devoted herbalist can use this year round to grow herb greens and small crops (such as cat grass) and to give belabored plants a boost in cold weather. For the more symbolic thinker, point a lamp with a grow bulb at a sigil drawn on a piece of paper to add a little heat to your purpose or to encourage growth—all the better if the sigil is placed on top of some potting soil for this process.

Colored Lightbulbs

Fans of color magic will love colored lightbulbs, but it's important to pay attention to some surprising safety warnings. Blue light requires special attention and careful use. While it can boost one's mood and is associated with reducing suicide attempts on train lines, excessive exposure to it causes the body to produce less melatonin and the short wavelength can cause migraines in those prone to neurological conditions. Limit exposure to blue lights to no more than an hour a day, especially in winter.

Significant studies have not been done on the effects of lights of other colors. But for safety's sake, when you use them, assume you will need a timer. You can purchase light timers at hardware stores as well, and their application can add some wonderful ebb-and-flow effects to the energy you apply to a given purpose.

For the most part, the colors of lightbulbs follow the common symbolic associations of a given color. There is another consideration here, however: every person has a different neurological response to color. This means that most people will have a strong color preference, along with possible color aversions. If you have a color aversion, don't use the corresponding colored lightbulb—your distaste for the color will, on an energy level, read as an aversion to whatever it is that color represents.

Here are some basic color references.

Blue: mood shifts, happiness, calm, focus, peace (but use this color sparingly)

Red: passion, intense focus, stimulation, strength

Green: healing, personal growth, opening the heart, emotional connection

Yellow: success, vitality, happiness, brightening, solar energy

Wires

Just as wires conduct electricity, they also conduct magical energy. Crafty Witches like to use them for wire-wrap jewelry, although traditionally this material comes from a jewelry or crafting supplier that produces wire for the express purpose of adornment. Wires are a great aid to crystal gridding. You can wrap wire around each crystal and form connections between the crystals of your choice, then set items within the grid that you wish to charge. You may want to use point-to-point energy transference, for instance, connecting citrine and quartz on either side of a CPU for a better processing charge. You can also use wires as a way of binding a lucky charm to yourself or to a business card.

Wires are a great aid to crystal gridding. You can wrap wire around each crystal and form connections between the crystals of your choice, then set items within the grid that you wish to charge.

Copper Wire

Copper deserves a special mention of its own because of its cleansing and protective properties. It costs more than most other types of wire, because heavy mining has made it an increasingly less common substance. An ankle bracelet made of copper wire wicks negative energy right off you and grounds it immediately. Gridding a rose quartz, amethyst, citrine, and clear quartz with copper creates a peaceful, protected space that can enhance focus and clear negative energy from almost any object. In addition, there are anecdotes about copper jewelry relieving arthritis pain and improving circulation.

Doors and Gates

Thresholds form the most powerful anchors of protective magic. It may seem a little strange to discuss using an actual door as a magical tool, but it is a way to add the benefits of threshold magic to a rented home. For some reason, owning the house to which a threshold belongs packs more of an energetic wallop than renting it. This may be because properties with owners on site tend to have less traffic or because of the centuries upon centuries of cultural importance placed on land ownership. If you can get a door—just so you own a door—it's worth considering. If space is a problem but you still want something to place house protection charms under, a gate can also work.

So what on earth does having a stray door do? It creates a threshold that you yourself own, no matter what. This forms a magical anchor that you can use in several ways, whether to create ritual drama by walking in and out of that particular door or to add storage or a display space for artwork and hanging knickknacks. Creating an altar around the door, and keeping it clean and dusted, adds a level of magical protection to your home that few renters typically enjoy.

To create that threshold safety, cleanse and bless the door as you would any other magical object. Smudge it, wash it, and anoint it with oil and tell it about its intended purpose in your home. Since it is a door, make it clear what you would like it to allow in—and what you would like it to keep out. You may want to go ahead and hang a protective talisman on it, such as a pentacle or an evil eye charm. An added advantage is that you need not bury ritual leftovers under any doorstep—you can simply place them in plant pots at the base of this particular door inside your home. You may also incorporate the door into your home as a means of storage, display, or concealment.

Hardwood

While marching out into the woods and befriending a tree is the most environmentally friendly way of accessing tree power, sometimes a slice of a board at a hardware store is preferable to braving a blizzard. Square tiles can serve as altar bases, and wood dust makes a fabulous rolled incense base. Hardwood dowel rods are a great foundation for wands, especially when combined with wire wrap or glue in order to connect crystals or other symbols.

Keys

While fancy skeleton keys get all the witchy cred, a plain old mass-produced house key or house key blank works just as well. Sometimes it works even better, because no one suspects the boring key.

Keys traditionally open things and protect them. Just as the athame can harm or heal, the key can close or open. This is both its purpose and its warning—be careful to think about what you open to, and think as much about what you lock out. You may want to assign certain keys to certain doors (whether or not those doors lock) as a way of accessing threshold magic.

Toolboxes

An eternal problem faced by practicing Witches is where to store the materials of the Craft. Since no one has, as of yet, opened a container store catering to Witches, we are forced to improvise. Fortunately, storage sheds, toolboxes, and cabinets work just as well for Witches as they do for plumbers—and really well for Witches who are plumbers! Those boxes with thirty tiny drawers can house small charms, herbs, or buttons. The larger boxes can hold smudges, ritual tools, and larger containers of herbs and powders. Cabinets can hold everything—and all the better if they hold everything well enough that you can read the labels with ease!

. . . .

Witchcraft is ultimately a discipline. To some, it is a religion. To all, it is a state of mind. While there is much to love about that state of mind when in a bookshop filled with wafting incense and shiny jewelry, sometimes a Witch's life takes us elsewhere. When that happens, it's important to remember that magic is everywhere and everything has an innate energy. Whether you're at a dollar store or a hardware store, looking at everything around you with your intent in mind and a good understanding of folk logic will unwrap a world of magical possibility. Your imagination is your most important tool of practice. Always bring it with you to the hardware store.

Sources and Notes

Cunningham, Scott. *Cunningham's Encyclopedia of Magical Herbs.* St. Paul, MN: Llewellyn, 1985.

Frazer, James George. *The Golden Bough: A Study in Magic and Religion.* 1890. Reprint, New York: Dover, 2002.

McKean, Cameron Allan. "How Blue Lights on Train Platforms Combat Tokyo's Suicide Epidemic." Next City. March 20, 2014. https://nextcity.org/daily/entry/how-blue-lights-on-train-platforms-combat-tokyos-suicide-epidemic.

"What Are the Effects of Blue Light Exposure on Our Health?" Blue Light Exposed. www.bluelightexposed.com/#what-are-the-effects-of-blue-light-exposure-on-our-health.

Diana Rajchel *is a Witch, psychic reader, and practitioner of the dark arts of community building. She has practiced Witchcraft for twenty years and cohosts the Youtube show* Psychic Witch Talk. *She is the author of* Divorcing a Real Witch *and a forthcoming Llewellyn title on urban magic. She lives in San Francisco, CA. You can find out more at http://dianarajchel.com.*

Illustrator: Jennifer Hewitson

Improve Your Concentration with Focal Jewelry

Lexa Olick

Not all of us can dazzle people with our wit, but a dazzling piece of jewelry can work just as well to stimulate some chitchat. A bracelet is a crafty conversation starter because it catches the eye and is another tool for us to use to identify ourselves. My sister's medical identification bracelet gives her peace of mind, and its modern, stylish design lets her bring awareness to women's health issues. I remember as a child, medical ID bracelets were only available in one basic design and my sister would never want to wear it because it made

her feel different. Nowadays, medical ID bracelets come in an endless variety of styles and my sister finally has one that she is proud to wear.

My mother was also on the lookout for some peace of mind and she found it in the form of a paracord bracelet. Paracord, or parachute cord, is a lightweight nylon cord that originally was used in parachutes and now is fashioned into bracelets that can be unraveled to use in emergency situations. My mother may never need this bracelet, but it makes her feel more secure just to know it's there.

My sister sometimes pairs her medical identification bracelet with silicone bracelets. These bracelets support many causes and their colorful appearance ensures that they are spotted and talked about. Bracelets have uses that extend beyond fashion and make them part of our identity.

For as long as I can remember, jewelry has always been more than just some shiny objects to me. Whenever I felt stressed or anxious in my youth, I could always reach out and touch an earring, twirl a necklace between my fingers, or rearrange the rings on my hands. I didn't need to see the jewelry to know it was there. I just had to feel it. Focusing on its presence brought me comfort, which boosted my concentration. The significance of the shape, size, weight, and texture of the materials that made up a piece of jewelry rivaled its visual beauty (as well as its ability to coordinate an outfit!). Relief was hidden in the shape of each bead, and all I had to do was touch it.

I started using jewelry to strengthen my concentration back in grade school. I felt a lot of pressure to do well in my studies, so stepping away from the computer screen was not always an option. I experienced carpal tunnel syndrome before I even hit middle school. Nevertheless, I only had to look to the fingers before me to find relief. Of course, it wasn't actually my fingers that caught my attention. My eyes were drawn to the rings that dazzled on each pinkie.

Working nonstop put so much pressure on my mind and body that it became harder for me to focus on the task at hand, but when I directed my focus to the silvery bands around my fingers, I felt like I'd hit a reset button. Simply rubbing each gemstone allowed me to focus on my breathing, clear my mind, and relax. In the end, I became more productive and tasks were easier for me to complete.

Stress and anxiety typically grow throughout adulthood as we're faced with increasing responsibilities, but jewelry continued to help me meditate. Just like my mother's paracord bracelet, keeping something around my wrist gave me peace of mind. The convenience of wearing a bracelet ensured that I would always have it with me. Jewelry would always be a comforting presence.

As a child, I didn't care what my jewelry was made out of. Whether it was plastic, pewter, resin, or silver-plated alloy, all that mattered was that I liked it. Unfortunately, there comes a time—or so I'm told—when we can no longer run around in junk-drawer jewelry. As we age, there is always someone in our lives, whether it's a parent, professor, or employer, who urges us to be more mature or look more professional. So sometime after college I had a garage sale to say goodbye to all my old belongings.

My front yard had a table that displayed all the accessories I grew up with. Each necklace, bracelet, ring, and earring had a story to tell. Most people might have grouped the jewelry by color, designer, or style, but I grouped them by their memories and sealed them together in plastic sandwich bags.

A young woman immediately went to the table with the jewelry and started fishing through the items. She pulled out a bag, opened it, and dug her finger inside. She held out a necklace by its clasp and told me that she would pay full price for just that single strand of beads. I told her she could have everything inside the bag, but she only wanted the necklace. She wouldn't take anything more. She told me that she wanted the middle bead specifically so she could make her own bracelet from it. My eyes sparkled at this information. We then continued to talk about jewelry, recycling, and crafts. This bracelet hadn't even been created yet and it still managed to spark a conversation. Delighted to find a fellow crafter, I gave the girl the necklace for free.

Although I was sad to see my childhood necklace torn apart, I was happy to know a part of it would live on. The young woman who bought it wasn't turned off by junk-drawer jewelry. What the necklace was made out of didn't matter to her. All that mattered was the single bead that called out to her. Perhaps years of being worn by a happy child had filled the bead with palpable positive energy.

I've participated in many garage sales over the years, but because I've always relied on jewelry as a tool to help me concentrate and unwind, I never sold another piece. The need to strengthen concentration or lessen stress is something people will never outgrow. So each bead, stone, and charm that I thought I'd outgrown was reinvented and refashioned into something new and stronger. I discovered that I could weave fond memories and pleasant experiences together to create new jewelry. Now, when I hold that jewelry in my hands and meditate, I can feel all that positive energy. That energy helps build my confidence and rids my body of stress.

Beads with a past help create meaningful jewelry, because each bead chronicles a part of your life. All those wonderful feelings are joined together. The piece of jewelry the beads create becomes a part of your identity. Gazing at the beads or feeling them with the pads of your fingertips is like reading a story. Each bead is readily recognized and brings you back to happier times. You can focus on jewelry to balance your breathing, calm an overstimulated mind, or break down mental and emotional barriers.

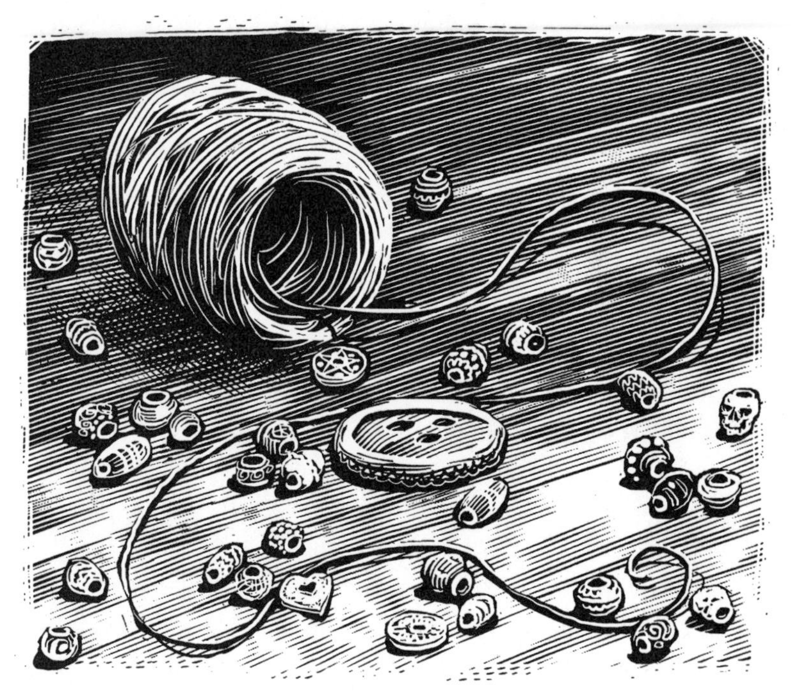

Create Your Own Piece of Focal Jewelry

To create a piece of focal jewelry, you will need as few as three components: string, beads, and a button. The most important part is finding beads that are important to you. You should choose beads that you can recognize even with your eyes closed. The beads should have a shape or texture that your fingertips can easily tell apart. When you can identify each bead simply by touch, it becomes easier for you to focus on your breathing and clear your mind.

Supplies

- .5 mm beading cord (at least 50 inches)
- Beads
- Button
- Scissors
- Bead caps and spacer beads (optional)

Step One

Take your beading cord and fold the length in half. This will double the cord and help create the clasp at the end. Elastic cord works great because it gives the bracelet a little more stretch, but I don't recommend it if you're using heavier beads such as genuine stones. Heavy beads will weigh down the elastic cord and make your bracelet floppy. If your beads need more support, look for natural fiber braiding cord, such as hemp or bamboo.

Step Two

With the folded length of cord in your hand, tie an overhand knot to fit the size of your button. Do not make the loop too tight or too loose. Try to make the loop the same size as the button. After you tie your knot, check to see that the button can easily slip through. The knot should be large enough to prevent the beads from sliding off, so you may have to tie several overhand knots on top of each other.

Step Three

Hold the cord together and begin to string your beads. Be creative with your patterns, colors, and materials. Try mixing faceted beads with smooth beads to vary the textures. Use different colored beads to symbolize emotions or wishes. Add spacer beads or bead caps to create distance between the textures and colors. They can help group and separate beads that hold different meanings.

Continue to string the beads. Feel your stress and anxiety melt away as you concentrate on the task. If you're recycling old beads, think about the memories they hold. Focus on your breathing and your intentions as you add each bead, and feel the energy within each one. The longer you handle the beads, the more focused you will become.

Step Four

Once you have finished stringing all your beads, secure them in place with an overhand knot. Thread the remaining cord up through the bottom of your button, then thread the cord back down the top of the button. Knot the cord together on the underside. You can add a dab of craft glue to the knot to help keep it in place. Trim off the excess cord. The button slips through the overhand knot from step two to secure the bracelet on your wrist.

Lexa Olick *is the author of* Witchy Crafts: 60 Enchanted Projects for the Creative Witch. *She has contributed to several* Llewellyn *annuals and is a graduate of the* University of Buffalo, *where she studied art and art history. When she is not writing or crafting, she spends her time traveling, gardening, and adding to her collection of antique glassware. She currently lives in* New York *with her family and several hyperactive pets.*

Illustrator: Tim Foley

Pow-Wow Magick: Make Your Own Charms and Hex Signs

Emyme

A golden safety pin, tiny jingle bells, a blue dolphin charm. Blank white paper, a compass and ruler, a pack of sharpened colored pencils. I invite you to join me on a journey into a small part of Pennsylvania Dutch pow-wow magick.

A few years back, I was introduced to, and quite intrigued by, this particular segment of our earth-based belief systems. Living in the Northeastern United States and being within a one- or two-hour drive of Lancaster County, Pennsylvania, all my life, I was naturally familiar with the various round signs adorning

many barns and homes along the roads in that area. Unfortunately, I was ignorant of the magick in pow-wow charms.

Here, I will address two elements of pow-wow magick that may be adapted to almost any earth-based belief system: charms and hex signs.

Charms

Charms figure in almost every branch of earth-based/Pagan/Wiccan traditions. For years I have created what I call Witch bags, or magick bags. I pack small fabric drawstring bags with me when I travel. Found items, such as feathers, stones, flowers, bottle caps, bits of paper, and leaves, all go into the bags to remind me of my travels and bring additional positive traveling energy. However, in these modern times, a bag—no matter how small—is not always the most convenient way to carry your good luck around.

My personal take on making charms of pow-wow magick begins with safety pins, which come in many sizes and colors. A perusal of brick-and-mortar craft stores and the Internet will reveal the bounty to be had. Indeed, you may find pins with special ornamentation specific to the charm you wish to create. Other options include fashioning safety pins with special designs or additions on your own, or using costume-jewelry pins. Should you choose costume jewelry, be sure the pin has a long, straight, pointed shaft on which to place the charms you choose.

As an example, you could use a large golden safety pin, with a flat charm of the sun affixed to the clasp and several smaller charms of flowers attached to the shaft. Attach this pin to another pin, which can then be attached to a garment, handbag, or backpack. And there you have a charm to encourage growth in a garden! The more advanced crafter (someone familiar with beading who has the tools) may also attach circular or lobster clasps to the baubles and beads. This enables use of both sections of the pin charms. Another option is what is called the French safety pin, or coilless pin. Charms can be affixed to the entire length of the shaft of this pin.

You have chosen your pins. Now for the charms. I've found the best place to begin your search is right back at any of the various

brick-and-mortar craft stores. At those national chain stores that sell any and everything you might need for any and every type of craft, you will find walls and aisles of packets of beads, charms, pins, and findings galore. Almost every time I have visited any of these establishments, there have been packets discounted. If they are not marked down in the aisle, they will surely be marked down in the clearance section.

I am very big on buying items on clearance. For the beginner, it is smart not to spend too much on your first attempts at making charms. When you get to a place where you are comfortable in your ability and can actually create what you see in your mind, then spend more on the materials. I have found packets of charms with letters, birds, flowers, religious symbols of all sorts, and beads and bangles of every color. Depending on the month, I have found charms with symbols appropriate for every season on the Wheel of the Year. Look for post-holiday sale items; bargains can be found for the following year.

I am very big on buying items on clearance. For the beginner, it is smart not to spend too much on your first attempts at making charms.

After visiting the large chain stores, you may wish to look for a specialty store. I am fortunate that there is a lovely store in the next town over that sells only beads and charms. If they don't have what I'm looking for, they are happy to help find and order it.

Finally, if you plan to gift your charms, purchase small organza drawstring bags. Every craft store carries them. The Internet has many options of color and size that may be bought economically in bulk.

So you have the pins, the beads, and the charms, but where do you keep all of it? Small items such as these need a designated place to live, all together. My space is a folding, water-resistant carrier designed to hold makeup and toiletries during travel. Slightly larger than a six-by-nine-inch book, it has several clear pockets with zippers for all the pins and charms. There are similar packets, carry-alls, chests, storage containers, and organizational pieces too numerous to mention that are available for purchase. Don't limit your search to craft stores;

hardware stores may have less expensive options—the sort of thing made for storing nails and screws and little bits of whatever it is that needs storing. Something as simple as small plastic bags stored in a shoebox will work too.

As with all magick, intention is the first and most important part of any charm you create. Use your imagination; it is not necessary to always be literal in your interpretation of what you wish the charm to embody. To enhance the work of my yoga instructor, I made a small charm that reads "coach," for she is a coach to the students in her classes. I also made a small dolphin charm to help bring the peace of the ocean to a friend who was grieving the loss of a loved one. And on every charm I make, I add at least one tiny golden jingle bell to attract the protection of the fey and their love of whimsy and cheer.

As with all magick, intention is the first and most important part of any charm you create. Use your imagination; it is not necessary to always be literal in your interpretation of what you wish the charm to embody.

Once I have fashioned a charm, I cleanse it with my breath to make it "mine." When I give it to the person for whom I have created it, I strongly encourage them to do the same, or to cleanse it in a mild saltwater solution and dry it thoroughly (or to use the cleansing method of their choice). The components of the completed charm have passed through many hands by the time the charm lands with the final recipient, so the charm must be cleansed completely to make it theirs so it will truly work for them.

With your supplies assembled and stored, now is the time for practice. Create charms for anything—let your imagination run wild!

These wonderful items can be taken apart and reassembled over and over again. The possibilities are endless. I have crafted charms for safe travel, for calm after a negative experience, for renewed health after an illness, for good weather, to heal a friendship, and to find a new job—and always, always with good intentions and positive energy.

Hex Signs

While doing some research, I was quite surprised to find that hex signs were not part of any ancient magical system but simply came into popularity during the fifties as part of the folklore craft phase—or not. There is more than one school of thought on this topic, and it is open to interpretation. What I discovered about hex signs brought to mind a similarity to totems, coats of arms, gonfalons, and family crests. Any of these items can be designed to suit the individual. The hex sign differs in that it may carry a little something extra, some additional magick, if you will, due to the insertion of elements from nature. Just as magick and miracles abound in our natural world, so does geometric symmetry. Leaves, flowers, spider webs, insect and bird wings...the list of symmetry in nature is far too long for this article. There is power in that construct, and that is where you should start when inventing your own personal hex signs. White is traditional for the background. All other colors should be dense and saturated, not pastel or translucent. This is another nod to strength of purpose, and it inhibits fading.

White disks of various materials and sizes can be found at craft stores. Less than a five-minute search on the Internet turned up cork, wood, and stretched canvas options, to name just three. The cork and the wood have to be painted white, but the canvas is ready to go. Another option is make your own circle with a round embroidery hoop and white fabric. Those of you who are involved in the fabric arts will surely enjoy this alternative.

Whatever material you choose, at whatever size, unless you are supremely confident in your abilities, I humbly suggest you create the design for your hex sign on paper first. Colored pencils, a ruler, and a compass are really all you need to begin. You may also seek and find round objects in your home to trace to make different sizes of circles. For a leaf pattern, trace an arc, then flip it over and complete the shape. A leaf-shaped button also works to ensure uniformity in design, and uniformity is important. If you are artistically blessed and able to work freehand, drawing consistent shapes will be no issue for you.

All the hex signs I have ever seen have one of two options: border or no border. I prefer a border, as it seems to hold the power of the sign in tight. No border lets the magic flow, which is good for a romantic or wedding hex, as the love flows out to all. The choice is totally one of personal preference, and as with all spells, intention is the first and main ingredient.

My foray into creating hex signs began with books. You can borrow or purchase a book about various symbols contained in existing hex signs. The Internet is one place to find examples of hex signs and other ideas. Your local library will no doubt have books on the subject, especially if you live within a few hours of the Pennsylvania Dutch of Lancaster County, as I do.

Once you have created your design on paper and are ready to transfer it to the permanent disk, paints are necessary. Again, a trip to the craft store will provide exactly the type of paint needed: finger paints. These paints are thick and ensure the required saturated color. No matter the brand, most of these are washable, so you will need to take care not to get the finished product wet. The upside is that the cleanup of brushes is easy. A coating of spray fixative will preserve the sign when you are done and the paint is dry.

Here is an example of how to create a hex sign for positive personal power, to promote success in your chosen vocation or avocation. I made a hex sign to enhance my skills as an author, with the hope that writing will be my complete source of abundant income in the future. First I drew two triangles, one atop the other, to create a six-pointed star. Three of the points are orange for career success, and the other three are brown for strength and to bring in the earth element for grounding and to reflect my star sign of Taurus. Around the border/edge I added a wavy black line with green leaves to symbolize growth and prosperity. The middle of the six-pointed star features a very simple stylized sun/moon circle in yellow and white for the aspects of male and female, flowing energy, and good health in general. This is the only part of my sign that is not symmetrical (however, it can be made so if you choose).

As is the case with charms, I cannot even begin to relate all of the design possibilities for hex signs. Love, marriage, health, prosperity, and protection are just a few. The main takeaway I got from my research is that hex signs should be simple, have symmetry, and reflect a positive personal intention. This is one magickal item I heartily recommend creating for yourself. To my mind, hex signs are different from charms in that you thoroughly imbue the finished product with your own spirit.

Hex signs should be simple, have symmetry, and reflect a positive personal intention. This is one magickal item I heartily recommend creating for yourself. To my mind, hex signs are different from charms in that you thoroughly imbue the finished product with your own spirit.

To review, first choose a topic for your hex, then research shapes and colors and their meanings. Obtain the supplies and create a pattern first on paper. Some people choose to bless all supplies before starting a project; that is up to you. After you have perfected the pattern, start in on the final project. Positive intention and a request for a blessing are in order, as is a final dry cleansing of the finished hex (perhaps a sage smudging). Hang your creation in a prominent place, one that will bring magick to the area in your life for which you have created the hex: a protection hex by the front and/or back door, a love hex in the bedroom, a good health hex in the kitchen, and so on.

. . . .

Charms and hex signs are but a very small part of the Pennsylvania Dutch tradition of pow-wow magick. Many books have been written about pow-wow magick. I do not profess to cite anything new here. This is merely what has worked for me.

Earth-based belief systems are numerous and flexible and adhere to one basic creed—*do no harm*. That is the most important part of any sincere daily spiritual routine. Imparting good thoughts and positive energy is paramount. Making pow-wow charms and hex signs is fun and creative and empowering. I send you blessings and wish you happy crafting!

Resources

Herr, Karl. *Hex and Spellwork*. York Beach, ME: Red Wheel/Weiser, 2002.

Phoenix, Robert. *The Powwow Grimoire*. CreateSpace, 2014.

RavenWolf, Silver. *HexCraft*. St. Paul, MN: Llewellyn, 1997.

Emyme *is a solitary eclectic who resides in southern New Jersey with her beloved cats and specializes in candle and garden spells and kitchen witchery. Apart from her full-time job out in the world, she writes poetry about strong women of mythology and flash fiction with a modern twist on traditional fairy tales. Emyme is looking forward to retirement and the opportunity to devote more time to her craft and her writing, and to the fresh challenge of moving from Mother to Crone status. Please send questions or comments to catsmeow24@verizon.net.*

Illustrator: Bri Hermanson

Voices in Your Head: Your Multidimensional Crew

Reverend J. Variable x/ø

I'm sitting down to write. It's 1:00 am. Everyone in the house is asleep, it's blissfully quiet, and I'm alone…

"*What are we working on?*"

"*Need a hand? I've got five extras.*"

"*Scooch over. I can't see!*"

"I WANNA HELP!"

"*Last time you helped, we ended up writing subpar imitations of James Joyce all night.*"

"*No hitting! Demerits!*"

Okay, so maybe I'm not exactly alone.

Some people have spirit guides; I have imaginary friends. I bet a lot of you do too, whether you realize it or not!

My invisible companions have been with me for as long as I can remember, and despite my parents' hope that I'd grow out of it, they're still around. They talk through me sometimes, or write, or draw, or help me build my websites. I think of it as an odd kind of channeling.

I used to feel weird or childish talking to imaginary friends long after I was supposed to have "grown up." Over the years, though, I've come to understand their true nature and the important part they play in my life. They've shared my best experiences with me, and they've been there during my darkest hours when I had no one else. More than once, my Others convinced me to keep going when I was ready to give up. Sometimes they help me a lot, and sometimes they need me to help them, but most times when they show up we just hang out. You know, like friends do.

If you're interested in cultivating a relationship with your own Others, I—er, *we*—have some tips and observations for you.

Where Do You Guys Come From, Anyway?

"*Well, I used to live on your plane. The last thing I remember was a really good party, and then I woke up on this side.*"

"*I used to be Italian. But then I found out I'm, like, from another planet. Ain't that cool?*"

"*We inhabit a dimension adjacent to your own, with a slight variation in the frequency modulation which—*"

"DAIRY QUEEN!"

It's a little different for everyone, I suppose. In our case, they're not me and I'm not them, but I've met some channelers who know that their Others are expressions of various fragments of their own personality. I'm sure everyone's description of the process is unique to their own needs and understanding.

I like to think that my Others are just a vibrational shift away, in a universe somewhat like this one (that's what they tell me anyway), and we just happen to be able to connect via the nodes and thin spots in the electromagnetic fields that form the planar membranes. Perhaps they're super-sentient thoughtforms, or *tulpas*: purposefully created beings that take on a life of their own. I'm a firm believer in the multiple-universe idea, so in our case, it's a little like making real contact with "fictional" characters. Everything you can imagine might be true in some universe, so why not?

I like to think that my Others are just a vibrational shift away, in a universe somewhat like this one (that's what they tell me anyway), and we just happen to be able to connect via the nodes and thin spots in the electromagnetic fields that form the planar membranes.

Opening Doors Between Worlds

You may have already met your imaginary friends. Were they around when you were younger? What happened to them? Did they eventually just wander away, or did they stick around on the sidelines, watching you grow up? Either way, they'd probably appreciate a call.

Maybe you're not on a first-name basis with yours yet, but you've been sensing some vague, unfamiliar sentience hanging around in your third eye's peripheral vision. Why not invite them to introduce themselves?

Mine often show up in my dreams and trance-visions, but we're also in touch throughout the day when I'm just going about my mundane business on this plane. It's mostly a matter of knowing how to listen—the running commentary from my external peanut gallery feels different from my own thoughts.

One way to meet your Others and get to know them better is to involve them in your hobbies and creative pursuits. Authors and artists tell of a magical point in the creative process when their characters take on a life of their own and commandeer the project: this is the "zone" you're looking for, when you realize that some of the thoughts and words flying through your mind aren't actually coming from you. Write stories about your friends' adventures, and include yourself in these tales! Draw pictures of them. Play music that you associate with them. Give them a turn too: let them write their own stories and create their own artwork (or music, or research projects, etc.) through you. Write messages to them and then hand over the pen and let them write back to you. Let them start writing to each other. Watch how the verbal style and even your handwriting change.

Don't overthink it and don't self-censor. It's not about producing a masterpiece (though it's nice when that happens). The idea is to find that place in your mind where your Others can get through. Plenty

of surprises will come out of your pens and brushes and keyboards if you let someone else borrow your hands for a while.

You might also find that you don't even need to use these tools as a medium for contact. After we'd been working together for a while through art and writing, my Others started popping right in and speaking through me. Have you ever watched an actor when their character starts improvising and throws the script right out the window? That's what this feels like. Again, it's not what I understand to be full-fledged *channeling*, since I'm always right there to step in (to make sure we don't startle my mundane-world friends…or get arrested). This technique can be intimidating at first, but once you all hit that groove together, it feels great to hang out at this level. The general public will never suspect that someone else was speaking through your mouth, and you're never going to see that shopkeeper or barista again anyway, so who cares if they think you're a little "off"?

If you're lucky, you might have a friend in this world who has Others too. This is when things really get interesting. (When I was in high school, my best friend and I would get on the phone every night and then just hand it off to our characters. Our baffled parents wondered what we could possibly have to talk about for hours at a time after spending all day together at school. They never knew that it wasn't us talking.) There's nothing like having a channeling partner and watching your Others get together, develop their own relationships, and create whole new storylines.

Caution!

There's a difference between invisible friends and true spirit guides. My Others aren't all founts of cosmic wisdom, though they come up with some pretty good ideas sometimes (and some pretty bad ones too). They're not disembodied voices in my head telling me to do horrible things. They don't take control of my body and cause trouble, and they don't suppress my own consciousness, like the entities in the minds of those who suffer from a multiple personality disorder.

As with any magical act, channeling your imaginary friends comes with some risks and responsibilities. Think about it: you're giving *other people* permission to borrow your body and brain. It's fun, but it's more than just a game. Once you open those doors in your mind, it can be hard to close them again. Channeling imaginary friends can be a rewarding, even healing, experience for all of you, but everyone involved has to acknowledge and honor the boundaries. Otherwise, things can slide quickly into dark, murky territory.

If you know that you're prone to imbalance, psychologically speaking, you might want to seek the guidance of a professional therapist as you begin working with your Others. There are counselors out there who recognize the value of this kind of activity and even encourage it. They can provide objective advice without judgment and can help you maintain a healthy relationship with your invisible pals.

It's easy to get entirely too wrapped up in your Others and their world. Over-immersion will cause trouble with your mundane life and relationships, so keep an eye on the lines between their personalities and yours. While you may all have a lot in common, your problems are not their problems, and their problems are not yours. If they become intrusive and won't leave you alone, or if you find yourself unable to function in the regular world without having them right next to you to step in at any moment, that's a red flag: you're getting in too deep. At this point, everyone needs to step back and review the rules. Declare a few days of solitude now and then to clear your collective minds and reground yourselves in your own lives.

It's easy to get entirely too wrapped up in your Others and their world. Over-immersion will cause trouble with your mundane life and relationships, so keep an eye on the lines between their personalities and yours.

Once in a while, too, you might encounter an Other who turns out to be a complete miserable pain. Just like the people you know in the real world, some of these Others are not always emotionally stable. What do you do about people like that when you meet them in this world? That's right! Just because you *can* communicate with an entity doesn't mean you *have* to. These aren't omnipotent deities that you have to placate. They're not all-knowing spiritual gurus who consistently dispense reliable wisdom. They might not all be humans, or even mortals, but they're fallible beings. Other-dimensional jerks are still jerks. Don't get so caught up in the excitement of contact that you let the control freaks walk all over you or your other Others. Real friends (imaginary or not) want to see you living well and happily and will treat you with respect.

As my long-time resident Nilly Rambus says, "If someone who moves into your brain-house turns out to be a GREAT BIG !?*@#!, you should sneak into their room and glue their underpants to the ceiling and put raw chickens in their pillowcases! And then They! Will! Leave!"

Disinfecting the imaginary linens and scraping the imaginary ceiling is a small price to pay for everyone's imaginary peace of mind.

Cross-Dimensional Collaboration

Now that you've started to form your company, what do you do with them? If the excellent companionship, entertaining storylines, and bad jokes aren't enough for you, try including them in your magical work. At one time, I had a small group of friends here in this world who were also familiar with their own imaginary pals. We used to cast circles with our Others, and after the ritual we'd spend many happy hours chatting with them via channeling or a ouija board. We're still in touch, but since we all live in different cities now, we've moved our cross-planar social circle to the Internet. Social media is an excellent outlet for channeled characters when everyone just wants to chat, and it's entirely possible to conduct magic rituals in cyberspace if you're comfortable working in virtual reality.

Your Others are handy advisors for daily decision-making, too. Even though they're not spirit guides, they can still help out a lot. Each character has unique talents, some of which can be harnessed by the channeler. (Nilly Rambus has a "psychic sniffer," and I'll sometimes ask him to come in and take a whiff of our location or a new person to see what his impressions are. He hasn't been wrong yet.)

On the other hand, you'll find that your Others often need your help, too. For example, one night I was working in my painting studio when one of my characters showed up, mumbling something about "art therapy." Knowing that he was working his way through some tough personal issues in their world, I turned the canvas and my hands over to him. We ended up collaborating on a series of intense paintings over the next few weeks. He says that helped him a great deal (he's since taken up painting with his *own* hands), and I got three new pieces that were markedly different from my usual style.

Invite your Others to help when you could use their perspective and skills in your own projects or problems. I don't have full access to everything my Others know, but their presence does tend to enhance my own abilities. When the tech geek shows up as I'm building websites, I don't instantly know how to write complicated code, but the search terms he suggests tend to bring up the information I need a lot more quickly. The psychiatrist and the shaman both notice things about people in this world that I don't necessarily see right away, and they help steer me away from unnecessary drama and heartache. The demon is an excellent "business partner," joining me for brainstorming sessions to generate new ideas for my freelance gigs and marketing campaigns. ("I *still think you should add soul-bartering options to your website's confounded payment system, my dear. The long-term interest will be worth a fortune in the afterlife.*") Okay, so not all of their ideas are going to fly in this world, but they're still a valuable team of advisors.

Once you and your Others develop a rapport, you might notice an increase in odd coincidences as you go about your daily life. It's not unusual for something that you were all just talking about to manifest somehow in this world: a line in a TV show, a song that fits perfectly, a newspaper headline that's just too specific to be ignored, or other little synchronous blips that make you go "hmm." I like to consider these events as little signs that the energy is flowing freely and the connections are strong between our worlds.

Just because your Others are imaginary doesn't mean they aren't real.

Reverend J. Variable x/ø *either is abnormally sensitive to signals from other worlds or has an imagination on steroids, or maybe a bit of both. On this world, it lives in Portland, Oregon, with an excellent photographer-husband and an assortment of small pets that don't make it sneeze. In the alternate universe, it resides with all its Others at a sprawling estate called Complex Manor, known to our neighbors as "That Great Looming Eyesore Down the Street Where All the Weirdos Live." Variable can be found online hawking psychic readings (some of the Others like to help with these now and then, too) and metaphysical geegaws at www.reverend-variable.com.*

Illustrator: Kathleen Edwards

Night Shift Magick

Gwynned Stone

As Witches, many of our spiritual paths assume that our lives revolve around a traditional work schedule. These paths are typically based on nature and cyclical occurrences, making it necessary for us to perform rituals and rites at particular times or on specific days. While we may make exceptions to our normal way of life for ritual, it becomes more difficult once our normal hours are reversed. Staying up late to perform a moon ritual is one thing, but staying up late for forty or more hours a week is a whole other issue altogether.

These days, more and more people are expected to perform their jobs beyond a nine-to-five schedule. Many of us work shifts at night that can prevent us from living a normative life and keep us from fulfilling our obligations and pursuing spiritual endeavors.

Not all right-hand-path practices require sunlight, but they are often associated with particular days and day-shift living. Covens and other groups often meet at times more conducive to daylight schedules, and even a solitary Witch can still be affected by these needs. Whether our spiritual path explicitly requires sunlight or moonlight, how do we keep our spiritual practice active while still managing our day-to-day life?

I have been on some form of night shift schedule for the majority of the past fourteen years. I've worked solstices, equinoxes, and holidays of all sorts, Pagan, secular, and otherwise. During that time,

I have been employed full-time, obtained two degrees, and tried to maintain my relationships with my friends and family. Some days keeping all that together while still trying to get a reasonable amount of sleep has been difficult if not outright impossible. Add a spiritual practice to that, and it isn't hard to guess which one is more likely to fall by the wayside.

So how can we incorporate our spirituality into our night shifts and even just our busy lives? Some of us, when faced with little sleep and mounting responsibilities, are forced to triage aspects of our lives in order to cope and survive from shift to shift. When we have to choose between sleep, family, and spirituality, it is often sleep that loses out, especially when our spiritual path feels like an obligation, either to ourselves or others. Sometimes we can snatch only an hour or two before we're up and helping with the kids or spending time with our families.

When we have to choose between sleep, family, and spirituality, it is often sleep that loses out, especially when our spiritual path feels like an obligation, either to ourselves or others.

No one wants to tell their children or spouse that they need to perform ritual rather than attend to them, and most people are likely to put their needs last when confronted with what they need to get done. Self-care, especially when dealing with hours that don't match our circadian rhythms, is also often neglected. We seem to forget that our physical needs often inform our ability to attend to our spiritual needs.

Even for those of us who don't have spouses or children, the night shift can be draining, and even alienating to a degree. When everyone else is out working, we're sleeping, or at least trying to. Rousing ourselves to work again can be isolating, especially if the only people we typically see are our coworkers (who statistically are not Pagan).

For many of us on the night shift, the most we can do is buy some blackout curtains and hope our families let us get some sleep before we have to get up and do it all over again. Then we stumble from our beds in the afternoon, try to find some way to keep up with our loved ones, and then go back to the job that allows us to care for our families.

Methods of Coping with the Night Shift

So, with all of this under consideration, what can we do to keep our spiritual practice going and not let it fall by the wayside? Although I can only speak to my experience with my own spiritual practice, some of these methods of coping with the night shift may be useful in managing your own.

When your spiritual path asks that a rite be performed at a particular time of day, consider whether the rite could be modified so you could perform it at a time that allows you to manage your responsibilities and needs. For example, if you have a summer or winter solstice ritual that needs to be performed at a certain time, you don't necessarily have to resign yourself to missing out on it. Instead, perform the rite when you can work it into your life. This is especially important, as most Pagan holidays are not acknowledged as holidays by some employers, which can make it difficult to get time off, depending on your work situation.

Another way to look at rituals is to view their times as relative. Just as you would eat lunch at noon on the day shift and eat it at midnight on the night shift, look at where you can mirror appropriate times. Instead of looking at these times as fixed, consider where they can be reflected in your current schedule for your needs.

But what if a ritual requires you to perform a certain function at a specific time of day? For example, if a ritual is supposed to be performed at midnight on the winter solstice, but you happen to be working that day because of the holiday rush and can't get it off, how do you still manage to observe the holiday while dealing with your work obligations?

In the past, I've tried to take my ritual to work with me and perform it on my break. However, I discovered an abundance of problems with this. Coworkers are an interference, obviously, but also the lack of ritual space kept it from being effective. Also complicating matters was the need to transport my sacred tools. I, for one, would not relish taking my athame or chalice to my place of employment. Even bringing my tarot deck is iffy, depending on my coworkers and my obligations for the night.

Another problem is that workplaces and work spaces are rarely tuned to the sort of energy that we need in order to perform ritual. Not only are they busy, frenetic places where one is expected to perform tasks unrelated to personal spiritual growth, but they often are not conducive to the quietude necessary for us to complete works.

Even when we leave work, much of the energy from it sticks with us and follows us home. When we have a bad day at work and we're already exhausted from the night shift, ritual becomes even more difficult to perform. This is why self-care should be considered one of the most important aspects when we want to participate in ritual and preserve our spiritual path despite working non-conducive hours.

A better option than trying to force our spiritual practice to fit into our daily life is to carve out some space and time intended solely for ritual. Whether this means taking time off on sacred days or finding a time for ritual that works for us, it is important to remember that ritual is often used to serve our spiritual needs, rather than the other way around. In order to make that space, examine what works best in your life from a holistic sense rather than an individual sense. If the particular ritual that you used on the day shift doesn't work with your night shift schedule, look for one that does. Find new ways to look at how you view the world and your place in it.

Asking our families for time to ourselves is often viewed as selfish, but sometimes we need time alone, not only to nourish our spiritual side but also to recharge and reenergize our relationships.

Ask your family and friends to help you with this. Asking our families for time to ourselves is often viewed as selfish, but sometimes we need time alone, not only to nourish our spiritual side but also to recharge and reenergize our relationships. Set aside a place and time for yourself and let your friends and family know when you would like them to let you have the solitude you need. Scheduling time alone is good not only for the spirit but also for the mind, allowing you the time to recover from stress and find your balance and peace of mind.

If you're working ritual with friends or family, be sure to convey your needs to them as well. I have found that many people who don't share their needs with their coven or family are often not understood when those needs become apparent. People often don't realize the toll that working nights can take on someone, physically, mentally, and spiritually, and a frank conversation can often lessen the difficulties that can arise from this lack of understanding.

Finally, one way to look at the night shift is as a way to challenge ourselves, to branch out into new ventures and ways of looking at the divine. Our spiritual practice should be constantly evolving, growing as we do. If we have grown comfortable with it, perhaps the night shift, or some other change in lifestyle, will help us grow not only as Witches but also as people.

Gwynned Stone *studies history, practices solitary Witchcraft, and works on her nonfiction projects while working the night shift. She is owned by her cat and lives in Colorado, where she adopts shiny spoons and dusty typewriters.*

Illustrator: Tim Foley

Attention Must Be Paid

Barbara Ardinger

In the great modern tragedy *Death of a Salesman* (1949) by Arthur Miller, Willy Loman, a traveling salesman, is engaging in some very strange behaviors. His wife, Linda, seems to be the only one who notices—or cares. "Attention must be paid," she says in act 1. He's "a human being, and a terrible thing is happening to him. So attention must be paid. He's not to be allowed to fall in his grave like an old dog. Attention, attention must finally be paid to such a person." (Just so you know, classical tragedy—the Greeks, Shakespeare, grand opera—deals with the deaths of kings. Miller's genius was to bring the classical dimensions of tragedy into the lives of ordinary people like Willy Loman—and you and me.)

What is the lesson of Miller's play for us Pagans? Who do we know in our "real lives" who needs to be noticed? To whom does attention need to be paid? What kind of attention?

Let's start by considering the psychological truth that we can't pay adequate attention to other people if we're not paying attention to ourselves. Attending to ourselves is not selfish behavior. We can't help others when we're not helping ourselves. Self-care means setting a good example for others as well as enabling ourselves to attend to others. So take a close look at yourself. To what part of your life must attention be paid? What needs to be attended to?

First, pay attention to your physical health. Make an appointment with your physician, chiropractor, optometrist, or holistic health practitioner. If they give you advice, follow it. If you don't get enough exercise, for example, start taking a daily walk or sign up for a yoga class. You certainly don't want to fall into your grave like an old dog.

Second, attend to your emotional and psychological health. If you need help, ask for it. My father always told me that if something isn't worth asking for, it's not worth having. This is good advice. Let's all follow it and ask for help when we need it.

Third, attention must also be paid to your spiritual well-being. Don't just be a lazy Pagan. Don't ignore the messages Pagans receive from unusual sources. Don't be the passive follower of some cultish leader. Examine what you say you believe and engage in honest conversations with leaders of your tradition and other priests or priestesses and scholars you respect. If you're a solitary, attend public rituals. Brush up your solitary rituals, too, to make them meaningful again. Don't just drift through the Wheel of the Year. Pay attention to

our eight holy days—and the days in between. What meaning do you find in each day? Pay attention to the moon as she moves through her phases.

When I started writing this article, I sent an email to a dozen of my friends and warned them that I would probably use their replies. I am happy to say that I have some very wise friends. Here is what one of them said about how we Pagans should pay attention to what it means to be a Pagan:

> *We can't just be Pagans on autopilot. We have to pay attention to our magical "muscles" and exercise them regularly. It's easy to go to the occasional ritual and call yourself* Pagan. *It's harder to remember that "magic is the art of changing consciousness at will" and to make magical changes.*

Another friend agrees with me that it's important to pay attention to the details and the moments of our lives. We should listen to our senses. That's how we find out what is important:

> *I think it's important to pay attention to the moment. In life, we see the forest, but very rarely do we look at the trees. We do not take in the details, and we tend to take the everyday things for granted. We need to pay attention and listen to our senses. On days when I really pay attention to the details, I feel the texture of fabrics and how they feel against my skin. I take time to taste my food more deeply and notice the temperature and how it makes me feel. I listen to music and let it touch my soul. I remind myself to be thankful for each and every thing and never to take anything or anyone for granted.*

Consider what my friends are saying. Let's not walk around on autopilot. Let's pay attention to what may be hiding inside what looks ordinary. Let's pay attention to the details of each moment. This kind of attention can, at a minimum, make daily life more interesting. We Pagans may look like ordinary people, but we know that the extraordinary lives in us, too. We also know, of course, that we won't attain perfection, but when we understand how attention must be paid to ourselves, we'll also understand how attention must be paid to other people.

Let's not walk around on autopilot. Let's pay attention to what may be hiding inside what looks ordinary. Let's pay attention to the details of each moment.

Look around you. Do you pay enough attention to other people? Life in the twenty-first century is so busy that, even though we can stay connected to our friends via our electronic devices, we may not be connected at all on the soul level like we can be when we're sitting in a real, live circle or even having lunch together. Do you sit down for meals with your husband/wife/partner and your children? Do you have real, spoken conversations with them instead of just gathering around the TV and watching football and reality shows?

In *Death of a Salesman*, Willy's sons invite him out for dinner, but then they meet up with a couple girls and abandon him. The son of his longtime employer fires him. He's abandoned by everyone in the play except Linda, and she's helpless to save him—which is why the play is a tragedy.

Attention must be paid to our family and friends. Take another good, steady look at, say, your coven or circle. Do you see the beginnings of situations that could become troublesome? What could you do to forestall these troubles? Who could you ask for help? What are your resources?

Is someone sending out tiny messages that are signals for help? The husband of one of my friends has been ill, and he also retired this year. Sometimes his conversations are hard to understand. But like Linda in the play, my friend is paying attention. Among other things, she's scheduling at least two outings a week. They go to museums and the theater, they go kayaking, they go out to dinner, and they go to meetings together. When this same friend received a scary diagnosis last year, she turned to me. I did some checking among my Pagan and metaphysical friends and received referrals to holistic healers and Reiki practitioners. My friend was happy with her physician, so I didn't challenge that. Instead, I took her to meet a Reiki master, from whom she received both healing and learning. She's paying attention to herself and to her husband. I think she's a good example of a real-life Linda Loman.

Yes, attention must be paid to our family and friends, including the animals that live with us. (Please note that we don't "own" pets. When you "own" someone, you've enslaved them. We live with our furry, feathered, or finny family members.) What action could you take to

help with any distress, major or minor? I used to live with two rescued Maine coon cats named Heisenberg and Schroedinger. When Schroedinger's kidneys failed and I had to have her euthanized, Heisenberg became very greedy for my time. When I adopted a new cat, he was jealous at first and started acting out. It took a few weeks—plus a few drops of kitty Rescue Remedy (no alcohol) in their water bowl—of careful attention on my part to help them become friends.

To what else must attention be paid? Pretend I sent you a note and write your own response to this question. Let your circle sisters and brothers and covenmates read it. Start a real, live conversation. Maybe create a new ritual about paying attention.

Here is another response from one of my friends. Do you resonate with anything mentioned here?

We need to pay attention to how we treat those in our lives....It's the small things—the way you greet and depart from someone, the way you handle snarls in traffic, the way you treat yourself. The energy we put into the big causes is usually positive and focused. We need to have the same focus when taking care of ourselves and those in our lives.

Many of us like to complain about people's dependence on their electronic devices. Who hasn't almost been run over by someone walking down the sidewalk and staring at their cell phone? How often have you seen people texting or tweeting or reading Facebook posts while they're supposed to be paying attention to traffic? Many people obviously believe that electronic attention equals personal attention, and they ignore the ways social media distracts us from paying personal attention to each other. One of my friends addressed this issue:

[*My husband*] *and I insist on an evening meal every night where we all put our phones down, but even the simple act of being able to watch a movie cannot occur without also watching or interacting with whatever is happening on our phones. My stepson will watch three and four television shows simultaneously, remote control in hand, while also watching something else on his phone.*

We Pagans always say we worship the ground we walk on. We like to say we pay attention to Mother Earth. We camp out and do outdoor rituals and commune with Mother Nature. But:

The fastest-growing spiritual group in the United States is the unaffiliated, spiritual not religious. Most of them cite nature as being entwined with their spirituality, yet they're not flocking to the Pagan movement. Why? Because they see themselves as modern and grounded in science. The Pagan elevation of the "old ways" doesn't appeal to them. The things most Pagans love about their faith—the gear, the dress, the rituals, the symbology—are what they like the least.

And this:

> I *think we should be more aware of our relationship with* Mother Earth *and how interconnected we are. Humanity has become so out of balance, and it just seems to be getting worse.* I *think* Pagans *have a responsibility to promote awareness of this connection in our communities, either through ritual, activism, or just in our daily lives.*

We Pagans need to pay attention to our communities, which may include those who came before us: our foremothers and other ancestors, our teachers and elders, and those ordinary, unknown people who carried our traditions into the present. We might want to create rituals to honor those people.

Willy Loman receives no honor at all until after he has sped into traffic and killed myself, and then even his funeral is inadequate. You and I can remember what Linda said—"Attention must be paid"—and honor ourselves, our communities, and our families, friends, and pets. What will you do to pay better attention?

Barbara Ardinger, PhD (*www.barbaraardinger.com, www.facebook.com/barbara.ardinger) is the author of* Secret Lives, *a novel about a circle of crones, mothers, and maidens, plus goddesses, a talking cat, and the* Green Man. *Her earlier books include* Pagan Every Day *(a daybook),* Goddess Meditations *(the first-ever book of meditations focusing on goddesses),* Finding New Goddesses *(a parody of goddess encyclopedias), and* Quicksilver Moon *(a realistic novel... except for the vampire). She is also well known for the rituals she creates. Her day job is freelance editing for people who have good ideas but don't want to embarrass themselves in print. Barbara lives in Southern California with her two rescued cats, Heisenberg (a Maine coon) and Schroedinger (a Turkish Van).*

Illustrator: Jennifer Hewitson

Witchcraft Essentials

Practices, Rituals & Spells

Building a Magical Meditation Practice

Melissa Tipton

There's no shortage of scientific data telling us how amazing meditation is for improving our mood, reducing stress, and even changing physical structures within the brain. But even armed with those facts, it can be hard to motivate yourself to stick with a meditation practice. As Witches, though, we have an extra incentive: meditation is a powerful way to ramp up our magical skills. Here are three ways to make meditation truly enjoyable, while reaping the benefits not only of improved wellbeing and brain physiology but also of enhanced magical power.

Working with Spirit Guides

In my personal experience, communing with spirit guides is downright life-changing. Before doing any spirit work, I like to create a sacred space by envisioning an energetic sphere around my body and stating three times, "My protection shield protects me from harm on all levels." Finish the third round with, "So mote it be." Set the intention that this sphere permits only beings who enter in perfect love and perfect trust, and spend a few moments tapping into a feeling of safety and security as you visualize this protection shield around you, fully charged.

Now that you have a safe space in which to make spirit contact, you can ask the spirit who is correct and good for you to make itself known. Be patient. In the movies this invitation is usually followed by a flickering of candle flames before all hell breaks loose, but in reality the experience is often much more subtle. Don't be discouraged if you don't sense anything out of the ordinary the first time—or the fifth. Make a commitment to keep showing up, even for ten minutes a day, making the invitation to connect. If you called a friend and they were busy and didn't pick up, you wouldn't give up and never speak to them again. The same rules apply here.

The other piece of the puzzle is learning how to perceive spirits. Your task during meditation is to remain aware and receptive. If you find your mind wandering, return your attention to something concrete, like your breath. While you are in this state of gentle focus, notice any sensations around or in your body, such as coolness or heat, a breezy or windy sensation (however subtle), or goose bumps. Perhaps the changes are more mental or emotional: thoughts might pop into your head seemingly out of nowhere, you might see images or flashes of color, or you might experience an emotion in the absence of any conscious triggers. All of these sensations can be the first signs of spirit contact.

Experiment with remaining aware and receptive and see if the sensations continue or increase. Then respond and see what happens. For example, you might ask a question, aloud or mentally, such as "Is this cool feeling on my hand a sign of spirit contact?" Remain still and wait for a response. Do the same with any new sensations that arise, slowly building your spirit communication skills.

If your intuition tells you that there is indeed a spirit attempting to make contact, but you are having trouble understanding, here are some techniques to try. As with any human relationship, you can ask for clarification. If you know you're a visual person, ask that the spirit show you images. If you're more auditory, ask that they speak telepathically or through other sounds. In my experience, not every spirit is able to communicate in all ways, but it doesn't hurt to ask. You can also experiment with automatic writing. Before going into meditation, have a stack of paper (number the pages so you can piece together the order later) and a pen or pencil at the ready. Rest the tip of the writing implement on the paper, close your eyes, and ask for messages to flow through you.

A pendulum is another tool that can work wonders when learning how to communicate with spirits. You can use a store-bought pendulum or make your own using a washer tied to a string. I've also used necklaces in a pinch. Ideally, cleanse the item before using it. You can do this by holding the item and visualizing it filling completely with white light. Begin by asking the spirit to show you a yes versus a no response. Sometimes a yes will be a clockwise motion, while a no is counterclockwise, but I have also had a yes response indicated by general movement, while a no is stillness. With the latter, I can feel the pendulum go energetically "slack," as if the power source has been turned off.

Regardless of how you choose to make contact, remember that as with human relationships, it's important to get to know the being on the other end. If you get an icky feeling, there's nothing wrong with ending the conversation. Maintain healthy boundaries, just as you would with a person, and allow trust to build over time. Also, just because a being is incorporeal doesn't mean it knows everything; use your intuition and good judgment before blindly following the advice of a spirit. Over time, you will build strong relationships with your primary guides, and they can help you "vet" other spirits that you meet.

Tarot Journeying

One of the most powerful ways to deepen your connection with the tarot is to journey into the cards' images. Whether you're completely new to tarot or a seasoned reader, you're sure to glean magical insights with this technique. Begin by choosing a card, and settle into your meditation position. Hold the card in front of you and gaze gently at the image. Begin to tune out all distractions as you focus on the card, letting your eyes flow from one part of the image to the next, following whatever captures your attention, from the bright color of a character's robe to a symbol in the foreground. Soak up the image, and when you feel ready, close your eyes.

One of the most powerful ways to deepen your connection with the tarot is to journey into the cards' images. Whether you're completely new to tarot or a seasoned reader, you're sure to glean magical insights with this technique.

Set the intention to journey into the tarot card in a way that is correct and good for you. Begin to call up the image of the card in whatever way works best. Perhaps the entire image will come into view slowly, or it might be easier to start with one feature, such as a character, and fill in the image around it. See the card's image in life size, and mentally project yourself into the scene. You might imagine yourself opening a door and stepping into the image, or simply reach out to touch one of the objects. Once you're inside, look around and interact. If there's a character in the scene, watch what they do. Ask them questions, such as "What are you reading? What does that symbol mean?" and so forth.

You can also ask if they have any messages for you, and if you are using this technique in the context of a tarot reading for someone else, you can inquire whether they have any messages for the querent. If there's an element of a card that you've always had trouble grasping, now is a great time to ask questions! This is especially helpful if there are cards that you inwardly dread seeing in a reading, either because of their negative connotations or because you always seem to draw a blank when you see them. Use this opportunity to get to know the cards, and your reactions, in new ways.

Be patient if answers aren't immediate; give yourself time to stay in the image, noticing any changes and receiving any messages. Once the experience feels complete, exit the image in the same way you entered (e.g., through the door, letting the image fade), and take a few moments to feel grounded and present in your body. It's helpful to keep notes from your tarot journey in a special journal that you can reference when doing a reading. I have found that the insights gathered in these meditations are an amazing supplement to any information I might find in a tarot book.

Symbol Walking

Symbols are, in themselves, a powerful way to connect with the unconscious and the divine, and meditation facilitates an even deeper connection. To begin, obtain or draw a representation of the symbol you wish to work with. Sit in your meditative position and focus your attention on the symbol, allowing all other distractions to gradually fall away. When you feel ready, close your eyes. Picture the symbol on the screen of your mind and set the intention to walk the symbol. Allow some time for an image to suggest itself spontaneously, but if nothing arises, experiment with one of the following:

- See an aerial view of the symbol in the form of a hedge maze. Project your awareness to the entrance of the maze and begin to follow the path, deeper into the symbol.
- Imagine the symbol created in sand on a temple floor, and feel yourself walking barefoot along the sand lines.
- Visualize the symbol as a crop circle, or a path circling a mountain, or a stream, or luminescent rocks creating a forest path.

As you walk the symbol, don't worry so much that you're tracing the shape precisely; trust the experience and give yourself time to notice details. Perhaps you encounter a bird in the hedge maze—introduce yourself and ask if it carries any messages for you. Notice any sensations in your body or emotions that arise; make a note of them when you come out of the meditation. These feelings can be used later to tap into the energy of the symbol. For example, as you walk the Reiki symbol commonly called Cho Ku Rei (aka the power symbol), you may get a feeling of deep serenity, which is one form of power. Later, if you are using the symbol in a healing, you can mindfully cultivate that feeling of deep serenity to reinforce the inherent power of the symbol. As with the tarot cards, it's helpful to keep a journal of your experiences, compiling your own personal dictionary of symbols.

I like to treat everything as a potential meditation focus. If I go hiking and a certain area resonates with me, I'll return to that place in meditation and explore. You can do the same with vivid dreams, returning to scenarios to glean more insights or to experiment with different outcomes. If a painting really sticks with you, visit it in meditation and ask for messages. These are wonderful ways to transform knowledge of the external world into knowledge of yourself, cultivating deeper wisdom. Meditation is your time for magical explorations and personal transformation—have fun!

Melissa Tipton *is a massage therapist, Reiki Master, and professional tarot reader who loves helping people discover their soul path through energy work and tarot. She writes extensively about happy living through yoga and Witchcraft on her website, www.yogiwitch.com. When she's not on her yoga mat or hiking Missouri trails with her husband, she's in her studio sculpting tiny food for her dollhouse miniatures business, the Mouse Market.*

Illustrator: Rik Olson

A Month of Ten Minutes: A Path to Embracing the Practice of Journaling

Susan Pesznecker

Before I begin, here's a full disclosure: I'm a college English professor in real life, and I'm also a writer and published author—so it's a fair guess to say I'm a big supporter of all kinds of writing. That said, I'm human, too, and just like most of you, I sometimes struggle with the act of writing. I find myself thinking I should write something but am completely stymied on how to begin. Or I dive into a writing project and find myself lagging at some point or hitting the proverbial wall, or even procrastinating about getting finished.

We magick writers... We're all human, too.

But that said, there's one aspect of writing I'm fierce about, and that's journaling. I've come to believe in the myriad ways it makes me a better writer, a better magick user, and a better—and more relaxed—person. I never skimp on journaling.

Journaling is perhaps the single most effective way to inspire your creativity, keep track of your life details, and, in the case of magickal folks, support your practice and craft. Researchers also know that journaling can help us manage stress, reduce anxiety, modify depression, and access deep memories (Holloway and Nelson).

Journaling is perhaps the single most effective way to inspire your creativity, keep track of your life details, and, in the case of magical folks, support your practice and craft.

Despite these benefits, if I had a nickel for every person I've talked to—student, magickal friend, apprentice, whomever—who's said, "I tried to journal, but it was boring" or "I couldn't keep it up" or "I didn't like it; I'd rather draw" or "What's the point?," well, I'd be living a nice life in a remote country.

In this essay, I want to convince you that journaling is worth the time and effort. I want to convince you to devote at least ten minutes a day to it. Ten minutes is a great place to start because it's a small, manageable goal. I want to give you ideas to make journaling work for you and to make it both practical and fun. I'll help you think about why and how you should try journaling, and then I'll set you up with a month's worth of ideas to help you put the practice to work. After all, journaling is like anything else: the more you do it, the easier it gets, and the more it becomes a routine part of your daily schedule.

I Dunno... Anytime I've Tried to Do Something Every Day, It Never Works

Let's take a pragmatic look at this. I'll assume you sleep eight hours out of every twenty-four. That means you're awake for the other sixteen hours. Ten minutes is equal to just 1/96th of those sixteen hours. That doesn't sound like much, does it? And it's not. I'm asking you to spend just 1/96th of your waking day practicing your journaling skills, and I promise you that if you make it a priority, you can find those ten minutes in your day.

Still not convinced? Consider that daily practice is all about creating a habit—i.e., the process by which a set of behaviors is repeated (and reinforced) until it becomes automatic. Developing a habit requires the following:

- Setting a simple goal
- Making a simple, focused plan to reach the goal
- Picking a reliable time and place to work
- Starting the plan and sticking to it
- Reflecting on your progress and on the value of the activity, typically by keeping some sort of record (like a journal, right?)

The goal? When you do anything regularly, over and over, you develop what physiologists call muscle memory. Your body automatically dives into the behavior and repeats it without thinking. The act of conscious reflection (e.g., asking what the experience has been like, how well it's working, what value it's had, and so on) helps further reinforce the behavior.

Some folks find that working with someone else helps keep them accountable. To be fair, journaling is an independent activity—you can't really do it "with" another person, but you can work side by side or perhaps share your progress with each other. I have a good friend—a fellow writer—who once a week goes to a "Sit and Write" group. During this time, everyone sits together in the same room for an hour and writes. That's all they do. No talking, visiting, or anything else is allowed. Just writing. They find that just being there together is beneficial. The act of gathering and writing silently becomes a habit, the community of writers helps them stay accountable, and the practice makes them write, which reinforces the activity.

You may not be able to arrange journal writing time with another person every day of the year, and you may not even want to. This business of journaling is a deeply individual process, after all. But you might choose to share your progress via social media or a monthly get-together with a fellow writer-friend. You might even join (or start) a writing group to share ideas.

Okay, I'm Listening. But I'm Not a Very Good Writer. What About That?

As a writing teacher, I'll reassure you that many people think they aren't good writers but actually do a perfectly wonderful job of writing. Have confidence in yourself: you have your own stories to tell, and no one else can tell them in the same way. Also, journaling isn't about being perfect. No one is going to see your work unless you invite them to, and there really aren't any rules at all when it comes to journaling. You can write bulleted lists, short paragraphs, or brilliant prose. You don't even have to write if you don't want to: you can sketch, paint, make collages, draw pie charts, or indulge in other creative approaches. If you like it and it works for you, it's good.

Do I Have to Write by Hand? Can I Use My Laptop?

For many of us today, written communication involves a keyboard rather than a pen. There are advantages to electronic journaling. It is easy and quick—many of us can type faster than we can write. E-journals take many forms and can be safely backed up on cloud sites, making them easy to access from digital device. They're easy to share and easy to search using keywords—versus thumbing through handwritten pages. On the other hand, with electronic journaling, e-distractions can be a problem, such as the incoming email or text message that is hard to ignore.

Many writers prefer using paper and a pen or pencil. There's a certain romance to setting pen to paper, and many find this more engaging and more magickal. Interestingly, research has also found that when we write by hand, we remember the ideas longer, understand them better, and retrieve them more easily than when we type (May).

What's the answer? Simple: choose the method you like the most and the one that works the best for you. The more you enjoy it and the more convenient it is, the more likely you'll keep it up.

But I Really Don't Like Writing. How Can I Journal?

As I mentioned earlier, there are other ways to keep journals besides writing. Journaling is all about capturing the details and ideas from your daily experience, and I'm betting you can think of many ways to do this. For example, you might try sketching, painting, or photography—or you might combine different forms.

One of my favorite approaches is to keep a nature journal. I'll write down my impressions from a nature outing or hike. I might add a quick map of the site or a sketch of a leaf or a cloud formation. Sometimes I'll glue in bits of brochures or materials picked up at the site. Later I'll come back and use colored pencils to add highlights or borders.

Your journal is by you, about you, and *for you*—no one else. The ways it benefits you are completely unique and in your hands. The sky's the limit, really. Let go and express yourself in whatever medium works for you.

Okay, I'm in. How Do I Get Started?

First, pick an ideal time. Don't try to journal when you're rushed or exhausted, and remember, *you only need ten minutes.* Find a time during the day when your mind is alive and alert. Be greedy about it: you deserve this time!

Second, if possible, pick a place where you'll be comfortable and undisturbed and where your materials are at hand. By journaling at the same time and place each day, you'll help the habit take shape.

Third, pick your materials and method.

Fourth, do it! Every day. For just ten minutes. (Of course, if things are rolling along, you can always keep writing!)

Fifth, reflect. Every so often, stop and think about how the process feels, how it's benefitting you, and so forth. Read through your past entries now and then, looking for discoveries or maybe for patterns that reveal something about yourself. Don't forget to journal about what you find.

P.S. If you miss a day for any reason, don't flog yourself about it. Just start again the next day.

A Month of Ten Minutes

You can use the following prompts and instructions to kick off your first month of daily journal writing, or create your own!

1. Get up early in the morning and greet the sunrise. Write about what you see and feel.
2. Write a prayer. Address a deity or energy focus, make a request, and offer thanks.
3. Sit outside under the full moon and "write down the moon," capturing your experience.
4. Where do you see yourself in ten years?
5. Write about your home and an experience you've had in it.
6. Reflect on a holiday experience with a friend or family member.
7. Write about a trip you've taken.
8. Describe your best friend.
9. Pull a Tarot card, rune, or other divinatory item and write or sketch about what comes to mind.
10. Create a sigil—a magickal symbol that represents you. Explain its meaning.
11. Discuss a color.
12. Write about a spell or charm that worked (or didn't).
13. Take a walk and look for a "day sign"—an occurrence that speaks to you.
14. Write about a magickal goal.
15. Where would you like to travel next?
16. Go back to your earliest memory.
17. Write about the current season.

18. Describe a favorite food.
19. Write a poem that captures your current emotions.
20. What is something you wish you could do better?
21. Pause and be mindful in the moment. What do you hear, feel, and see?
22. Describe a memorable ritual.
23. Write about your favorite season.
24. Write a meditation. Then use it!
25. Write about a question, discussion, or controversy in your magickal community.
26. Write about the moon.
27. What is the most important magickal tool?
28. Do you have a spirit animal? What is its significance?
29. Imagine looking into a scrying bowl. What do you see?
30. Who is your hero?

Here's wishing you a great experience with your journal!

Works Cited

Holloway, Beth, and Gail Nelson, medical reviewers. "Journaling for Mental Health." University of Rochester Medical Center. www.urmc.rochester.edu/encyclopedia/content.aspx?ContentTypeID=1&ContentID=4552.

May, Cindi. "A Learning Secret: Don't Take Notes with a Laptop." *Scientific American*. June 3, 2014. www.scientificamerican.com/article/a-learning-secret-don-t-take-notes-with-a-laptop.

Recommended Reading

Didion, Joan. "On Keeping a Notebook." In *Slouching Towards Bethlehem*. 1968. Reprint, New York: Farrar, Straus and Giroux, 2008.

Pesznecker, Susan. *Crafting Magick with Pen and Ink*. Woodbury, MN: Llewellyn, 2009.

Susan Pesznecker *is a writer, college* English *teacher, nurse, practicing herbalist, and hearth* Pagan/Druid *living in northwestern* Oregon. *Sue holds a master's degree in professional writing and loves to read, watch the stars, camp with her wonder poodle, and work in her own biodynamic garden. She is co-founder of the* Druid Grove *of* Two Coasts. *Sue has authored* Yule, The Magickal Retreat, *and* Crafting Magick with Pen and Ink. *Visit her on her* Facebook *author page (www.facebook.com/usanMoonwriterPesznecker).*

Illustrator: Kathleen Edwards

Witchy Spa Day

Calantirniel

Who among us healer types doesn't need a day of rejuvenating downtime? So, surfing around the Internet has given you some ideas for a DIY stay-at-home spa day. But you may want a routine that not only includes goodies for eating, bathing, and pampering but also makes room to inspire and uplift your soul and spirit. First decide if you will be alone or with another (such as your significant other or a friend). Giving a massage to each other is infinitely better than self-massage, but it may be easier to enjoy the downtime to go inward alone.

Gather Your Supplies and Prepare Your Day

Unplug! No phone, no Internet... you are on a mini-vacation! Turn off your phone and computer notifications or at least turn down the sounds or lights, and consider placing some black tourmalines around your Wi-Fi areas to deflect EMFs (electromagnetic fields). Have lots of spring water and lemons on hand, as well as herbal teas and fruits and veggies to make a morning smoothie. Eat lightly but nutritionally and organically, avoiding the usual offenders: sugar, sugar substitutes, wheat/gluten, and most animal-derived foods. Consume good fats sparingly, including olive oil, avocado, coconut, and grass-fed butter. Stevia, raw honey, and unsweetened, organic active-culture yogurt are allowed, and use Himalayan pink salt for mineral balance. Some of the suggested foods can double as yummy body treatments!

Sometimes I drink a warm cup of fennel tea the night before, or a stronger yet gentle blend that works on the colon, to move things through my system and get a head start on a slow detox. Pampering is the key, not suffering. Also, try to use what you have on hand—modifications are liberally allowed!

Your Awakening

If you remember your dreams, write them down. Journaling is a wonderful activity for spa day. You can then explore what these dreams may mean using your intuition or a dream dictionary. If you meditate or do a morning ritual/reading, this is a good time for that.

The best time for exercise is usually after awakening and before eating. Yoga or belly dancing are wonderful! Drink some water with lemon in it beforehand. If you don't have a yoga book or DVD, you can always use YouTube to find a plethora of workouts. Or just do a series of simple stretches and take a brisk walk outdoors. Get your circulation going, and don't overdo it if you usually don't exercise.

For breakfast, it's green smoothie time! Put some kale or other greens in a blender, along with some pineapple, mango, passion fruit, or any type of berries, as well as some water or unsweetened, organic fruit juice of your choice—yum! You can add some raw apple cider vinegar, herbal powder (such as maca root), or pre-brewed herbal tea for more physical healing, and add some flower essence drops for emotional healing, too. If you want organic coffee, brew and drink this first and wait at least thirty minutes before making your smoothie, as coffee affects nutritional absorption. Save your coffee grounds for a wonderful face/body treatment.

Mid-Day Activities

Go on an outing of your choice. Being out in nature is perfect—go to a beach, park, or hiking trail in your area. Or, alternatively, wind down indoors with a good book, or make a trip to your favorite metaphysical shop, art museum, or antique store. Do whatever uplifts you and is something you usually don't make time to do for yourself. Bring your oracles with you, or splurge on a professional reading. If you feel like it, bring home fresh flowers. You can smudge your whole house with sage or sprinkle water and a salt circle around your property to spiritually revitalize your sacred space. You may wish to stay home and create a vision board for your life and goals. Use photos from old magazines, calendars, or real estate catalogs, and glue images or positive word phrases to cardboard and hang in your view—and know this will manifest very powerfully!

You may wish to stay home and create a vision board for your life and goals. Use photos from old magazines, calendars, or real estate catalogs, and glue images or positive word phrases to cardboard and hang in your view—and know this will manifest very powerfully!

Prepare a light lunch, perhaps some ginger miso broth with tofu cubes, green onions, and fresh parsley. Or snack on rice crackers and garlic hummus, or blue corn chips with fresh salsa. A green salad with a drizzle of olive oil and lemon or wine vinegar with herbs is another great choice, or go out for a healthy lunch.

This is a great time for a massage. You can spoil yourself with a professional one, or place a few drops of releasing essential oils in ½ to

1 ounce of coconut oil and massage yourself (or your partner—take turns). Ylang-ylang and juniper oils work well. If you can't do a full-body massage, a hand or foot massage using reflexology techniques or a neck and shoulder rub can do wonders! Allot thirty minutes to an hour for each person, or do the massage after applying a face mask and hair oil—your choice.

Face Mask

To make your own face mask, combine the following ingredients:

- 1 teaspoon yogurt
- A small drizzle of raw honey
- Some wet coffee grounds (or ground old-fashioned pressed oats)
- The juice or mashings of your favorite fruit or veggie (such as lemon, cucumber, papaya, pineapple, or peach)
- A pinch of crushed green tea, peppermint, chamomile, rose petals, or dried ginger/cinnamon
- A bit of coconut oil
- A drop of your favorite essential oil(s), no more than three (lavender, geranium, and rosemary are favorites)

Be flexible and use what you have on hand. Mix the ingredients together and test for sensitivity first by placing some of the mixture on the inside of your wrist for a few minutes. Then apply the mask for twenty to thirty minutes, or set in the fridge if you are going to apply other treatments so you can relax all at once before rinsing and—my favorite—bathing! As an added bonus, place sliced cucumbers or moistened tea bags under your eyes. (Drink fresh parsley tea for black circles.)

Body Scrub and Scalp Massage

This body scrub is fantastic for reducing cellulite, softening stretch marks, and bringing wonderful tone to the skin. Combine the following ingredients:

- ½ cup wet coffee grounds (perhaps from your morning coffee)
- ½ cup Epsom salts
- Grapefruit or lemon juice (grate some peel, too, if you can)
- ¼–½ teaspoon dried ginger
- Softened/melted coconut oil
- 10–15 drops total of grapefruit, cypress, juniper, and/or rosemary essential oils (optional)

Once again, test for sensitivity first by placing some of the mixture on the inside of your wrist for a few minutes. This mixture is messy, so mix and apply it either outside or in the bathtub, over some newspaper or a drain catcher. (Don't let it go down into the plumbing, although it's okay to put it in the soil to nourish your plants.) Drink some lemon water and allow the mixture to stay on your skin for twenty to thirty minutes.

Meanwhile, take a few drops of coconut, olive, avocado, or your favorite oil and rub between your hands. Apply the oil to your scalp and massage well, running your fingers down to the ends. Another option, if you are a blonde, is to combine some yogurt, chamomile tea, and lemon juice and apply the mixture to your hair. If you are a brunette, make some strong sage or rosemary tea, then cool and apply to hair. Rinse off outside or, if in a tub, rinse into a drain screen/filter and place the remains in the compost or trash.

Bath Soak and Hair Treatment

Light your favorite spellwork candles and place them in fireproof areas, then place flowers in view, if you like. To make your own bath salts, gather the following ingredients:

- 1 cup Epsom salt
- ⅔ cup baking soda
- ⅓ cup sea salt or table salt (optional)
- 10–15 drops of any blend of essential oils (my favorite blend is orange, sandalwood, orris root, and patchouli)

Combine the first two (or three) ingredients. Then mix in the essential oils to make your own bath salts.

Next, rub yourself down with a little coconut or olive oil, if needed. Then add *almost* all of the bath salts to a tub filled with the warmest water you can stand, and soak. Allow all your troubles and any muscle aches and pains to melt away. Run more hot water if it starts to get cold. Soak for thirty to forty minutes, without turning into a prune! Do your spellwork, affirmations, or switchwords, or listen to meditations or healing, intuitive, or motivational material (such as a smoking cessation program or any specialty you wish).

After draining the tub, wash and/or condition your hair with the most luxurious natural products you have. Then pour over your hair (but don't rinse out) a rinse consisting of raw apple cider vinegar in warm spring water. (I usually use 1–2 tablespoons raw apple cider vinegar with 16 ounces warm spring or distilled water—less vinegar for oily hair, more for hair needing moisture.) Use the rest of the bath salts to wipe down the whole tub area, which cleans the tub and smells amazing! If you can, let your hair dry naturally after you comb it, to give it a break. Apply your natural body products (deodorant, facial toner, moisturizer, eye oil) and either do a manicure/pedicure and get dressed/made-up for going out later, or, if you want, drink some more lemon water and take a nap. No rules—it's your day!

Winding Down

For dinner, prepare some basmati rice and stir-fry some veggies in coconut oil or ghee and add curry/chai seasonings, or use a prepared masala sauce. Serve with lemon-yogurt sauce with cinnamon, cumin, and black pepper (add a tiny amount of stevia or raw honey to taste, if desired). Or try gluten-free curly pasta made of brown rice and quinoa, with organic tomato basil sauce seasoned with more fresh basil and Himalayan pink salt, along with a side salad and your favorite homemade dressing. Have a wonderfully decadent yet healthy dessert, such as blueberry raw cacao coconut cream pudding.

At bedtime, wind down with a book and a warm cup of relaxing herbal tea sweetened, optionally, with stevia. If you didn't get a reading or trade readings with another, get out your favorite divination tool (such as tarot cards, runes, ogham, a card oracle, or the I Ching) and perform a short-term reading for what you need to know now, as well as a long-range reading for knowing what themes are forthcoming in your life, then write about them in your journal.

Create a sacred circle for yourself. Ask for all of your guides to be present, and optionally call your working circle in whatever way you wish. Ask to be grounded to the earth, allowing energy to flow up from your feet and over your head. Ask the cosmos to enter through your crown and meet the earth. Then properly activate and balance each chakra. Fill your aura with this clean energy, dissolving and releasing old energies no longer needed down your grounding cord, which goes from your root chakra to the center of the planet and to the source. Know you are protected as you prepare to ask for guidance. Developing your intuition and learning to trust spiritual messages can help you navigate through life. Make plans while remaining open for the right opportunities (and compare with your vision board!).

Sweet dreams! You had a blissful day of nourishing and much-needed self-care. Have a DIY spa day seasonally, if possible. Carrying over good habits into your daily life helps too—enjoy!

Calantirniel (San Diego, CA) *has been published in nearly two dozen Llewellyn annuals since 2007 and has practiced many forms of natural spirituality for two decades. She is a professional astrologer, herbalist, tarot card reader, dowser, energy healer,* ULC *reverend, and flower essence creator/practitioner. She recently realized that her most marketable skill is an uncanny sense for utterly precise event timing. She is creating a membership-subscription e-course website to teach other intuitives these timing skills. She is also a co-founder of* Tië eldaliéva, *meaning the* Elven Path, *a spiritual practice based upon the Elves' viewpoint in* J.R.R. Tolkien's Middle-Earth *stories, particularly* The Silmarillion. *Please visit* IntuitiveTiming.com.

Illustrator: Tim Foley

How to Create an Altar for Every Room or Space

Dr. Alexandra Chauran

Altars are often an essential part of a Wiccan's practice. I'd like to share with you some tips and lore surrounding altars and provide some inspiration to create permanent or semi-permanent altars in your living space, your workplace, your garden, or even your car. I find that having a touchstone close at hand can help visually remind me of my commitments to my deities and my ability to find peace in my connections with them.

Why keep altars in the first place? Aside from being a place to hold all the necessary components for rituals and magic, altars are prayers made manifest

with tangible mementos as well as spiritually useful and esthetically pleasing objects. Think of an altar as a curio cabinet that is working hard to change your inner and outer lives. It can be a place for you to sit and meditate, pray out loud, or simply place your mortgage bill in the hope that the bill will be paid.

Some people gravitate naturally to altars. There are social media communities full of people showing off their own beautiful altars with pride, or even posting photos of interesting altars that have seemingly been found in the wild. At significant locations around the world, backpackers, climbers, and other tourists leave small tokens to signify their respect for the space, essentially turning a statue or a beautiful view into an altar. When I first walked into one therapist's home office, I noticed that she had beautiful little altars everywhere. A selection of crystals lined a banister. A bowl of water with some seashells accenting it sat on an end table. A pile of smooth stones drew attention toward art on the wall. Such did they appeal to the elements of water and earth that I asked her if she was Pagan. It turned out that she was not Pagan at all, but that just goes to show how altars can bring peace and a sense of meaning to any home.

Types of Altars

An altar can be set up just about anywhere. A round or rectangular table in a spare room works just as well as a card table set up outdoors or a flat rock in the woods. Various magical tools and decorations can be placed upon the altar table. Many altars can be easily broken down for transport or storage until the next occasion for ritual.

You can create an altar for any room or space. Here are some ideas.

Family Altar

Aside from the altar in the temple room in my home, in which I perform rituals with my coven, the most visible altar I own is our family's altar. The family altar is the first thing that one sees when walking in through the front door. I placed deity statues on the altar, dividing it up roughly into the four elements. North is for objects representing earth, such as stones, while south is for things representing fire and is where I typically burn a candle. East is for things that represent air and can be a good place for incense. West is for water and can be a good location for a bowl of water or even a snow globe.

Your family can join in on the fun. I allow my kids to place their favorite rocks, flowers, acorns, abandoned snail shells, art, and more on the altar. The family altar can be a place to pause and pray. We redecorate it for the seasons. At Yule, the family altar becomes a place to set a small Yule tree and other holiday decorations. When Ostara rolls around, the family altar is replete with pysanky eggs. During the spring, the altar is festooned with flowers. The living and changing nature of the altar makes it a wonderful way to bring worship into your life.

Workplace Altar

An altar in the workplace must usually be more discreet than one at home. You can carve out space for an altar on a shelf, in a corner of a cubicle, or even in a drawer. Try the elemental organization that I just described, or simply add relaxing things to your altar space that can act as touchstones when you're feeling stressed and need to reconnect with your spiritual strength. A small Japanese sand garden can act as a workplace altar, and is indeed seen commonly in the workplace. If you have the opportunity and space to use a plug-in fountain, the running water can add a little bit of peace to an otherwise stressful day. Covert or abstract images of deities can be welcomed even in a secular workplace. Who's to say whether a beautiful print of Aphrodite rising out of the sea is merely art or is a focus for worship? I know one reader of mine who created a beautiful fairy garden at work. If you have enough light in your workspace, a garden full of tiny plants and statues of fairies can bring a bit of the magic of the outdoors to even the most dismal work environment.

An altar in the workplace must usually be more discreet than one at home. You can carve out space for an altar on a shelf, in a corner of a cubicle, or even in a drawer.

Car Altar

I do have a small altar in my car that is not distracting. I placed it there after a terrible accident that my children and I survived. I had a necklace of rowanberries hanging from the windshield for protection, and the crumple zone stopped exactly there.

To assuage my anxiety after the accident, I added to the spiritual protection of my car. I bought a pentacle window cling to symbolize the protection of the elements and spirits. I found a small pendant online that spoke to me that pictured both the Goddess and the God. I snapped off the loop made for hanging and used some solidifying putty on the back to create a statue out of the pendant. I then glued the pendant and a small bud vase made for cars off to the side of

my dashboard, so it would be out of the way. As luck would have it, there is a tiny drawer there (possibly originally intended for loose change) that is now a place to put trinkets, stones, and other small offerings to my gods.

When creating a car altar, be careful not to obscure your vision or inhibit your ability to move your arms and hands. Always pay homage to your car altar before or after your drive, not during. Even at a stoplight you should remain aware of the traffic around you.

Ancestral Altar

You don't have to build an altar to the elements or to deities. An ancestral altar can be a way to keep in touch with those who have passed away. Typically, ancestral shrines are decorated with photos of the deceased. Be careful to use photos only of those who are already dead. If there is also a living person in the photo, crop that living person out so that you can give proper and sole honor to those mighty dead who are in a position to offer you aid.

The focus of ancestral altars is often on offerings. Dedicate a cup to your ancestral altar and use it only for that purpose to keep your intentions pure. A tiny bit of your ancestors' favorite foods can be placed on a plate on the altar and left for a day or more, depending on how quickly it might get rancid. Don't worry if a pet takes off with some of the food, as they are acting as a proxy for your ancestors. Make sure you don't put out offerings that are dangerous to any pets or small children who may be wandering around in your house. Try to put out a little bit of food that you know your deceased loved one would enjoy. If you have no idea what your loved ones might have enjoyed, try a food from their nation of origin or the location in which they grew up. Typical liquid offerings to ancestors include alcohol, milk, or simply water.

Dorm Room Altar

I wanted to include some special tips for altars in places where things like flames, incense, and pointy items (such as athames) are not allowed. Someday you might find yourself in a space such as a dorm room or hospital room in which your ability to stock your altars is limited. Incense can be replaced with feathers in a lovely vase or even with a bubble solution. Amber incense or essential oils smell lovely even when they are not being burned, and can be put on display. As for candles, there are lovely LED light options that sometimes even flicker like real candles. I've even used glow sticks in outdoor rituals in a pinch. You can use sketches and drawings to create deity imagery. Use your imagination, because if all else fails, your mind is the only tool you need to create an altar on the astral plane. Simply close your eyes and imagine all of the tools and calming images that you would put on your altar.

Altars in Any and Every Room or Space

Every room can have an altar. Imagine an Aphrodite shrine in your bathroom. A bowl, some beautiful rocks and shells, and perhaps a statue are all you need for a lovely shrine. As you look around your home, think about the elementals associated with each space that could hold an altar. For example, if you have a nice shelf on a south wall, you could find a wonderful candle sconce to honor the element of fire, and add a picture of a fiery piece of art that reminds you of the divine. If you have space on the top of an appliance or a piece of electronic equipment to the north, try putting a potted plant and a selection of beautiful stones that speak to your spirit there.

Each room could have four or more elemental altars, if you desire, but you don't have to go overboard. Look at each room with a critical eye and think about where you spend your time. It would be nice to have an altar that you can pass by every day or glance at when you're in between tasks, rather than too many altars that will end up gathering dust.

How to Use Your Altars

You can use your altars as little or as much as you like. You can spend just a moment touching an altar as you enter your home to ground yourself and welcome yourself to your happy space, or you can seat yourself in front of your altar for hours to pray and meditate. You can perform rituals around your altars alone or with loved ones. The benefits of altars are numerous, and the more the merrier.

Dr. Alexandra Chauran (Issaquah, WA) *is a second-generation fortuneteller, a High Priestess of British Traditional Wicca, and the Queen of a coven. As a professional psychic intuitive for over a decade, she serves psychic apprentices and thousands of clients. She received a master's in teaching from Seattle University and a doctorate from Valdosta State University, and is certified in tarot. In her spare time, when she's not teaching students of Wicca, she enjoys ham radio with the call sign WI7CH. She can be found online at SeePsychic.com.*

Illustrator: Jennifer Hewitson

Spiritual Communication 101

Deborah Castellano

The idea that you could (sometimes literally) hear a goddess speak to you was incomprehensible to me when I first became a Witch. I was brought up Catholic, and prayer always seemed to require a lot of tedious repetition and waiting—and never, ever getting mad at God for failing to deliver ponies, boyfriends, good hair, or extra trips to the library. Getting pissy with God meant that you doubted her plan, that you weren't patient and were possibly faithless. Also, God is very busy and she doesn't have time to fulfill every boring little request you put in.

Even on the best of days, I was a far cry from the teenage-girl Catholic saints I liked to read about. I got restless from being on my knees too long, I didn't want to fast, I cussed a lot, and I got into cars with boys. Few people would describe Catholic Teen Deb as pious, though I was as faithful as I knew how to be.

When I became a Witch, it took some time before I met people who had two-sided conversations with goddesses and spirits. It took me a while to trust that voice, because if hearing voices was not a sign that a long and prosperous life was on the horizon even for Joan of Arc, I didn't think it would bode terribly well for me either.

I'm still not one of those people who receives verbal messages from goddesses and spirits all that often. This can be frustrating, because if the people around you who practice magic receive messages this way, you start to wonder whether you are *doing it wrong*. You feel like if you just tried harder, your magic would work like the majority of the occult population's magic appears to work.

But your magic is your magic, and it's going to work the way it's going to work. Just because most books about practicing magic tend to focus on visual thinking doesn't mean you can't practice magic if you're not a visual thinker. Maybe singing works for you, or dancing, or sketching. Maybe working with a friend and collaborating works for you, or maybe you work best by yourself. Maybe looking at magic like a logic problem works for you. If you find a method to do Witchcraft and it works, then that is the right way to do it.

Just because most books about practicing magic tend to focus on visual thinking doesn't mean you can't practice magic if you're not a visual thinker. Maybe singing works for you, or dancing, or sketching. . . . If you find a method to do Witchcraft and it works, then that is the right way to do it.

For me personally, my indicators that my Witchcraft is working tend to be more along the lines of radiomancy, the Golden Moth Illumination Deck (which has a very free-form interpretation system), and sometimes dreams. My sister, who is generally thumbs-down on all magical experiences regardless of spiritual background, is actually more attuned to the other side of the veil than I am, which is every bit as annoying as it sounds.

How to Win Spirit Friends and Influence the Universe

Here are some things to consider when communicating with spirits.

Who Is Initiating This Conversation?

Sometimes, when a goddess or spirit is interested in you, much like when a corporeal person is interested in you, they give you little signs: a small bit of good fortune with something that symbolizes them, seeing and hearing about them everywhere, a dream with them in it, and so on.

If you are not that into them, you can keep hitting "ignore" until they get the message—which works the same way as it does with other people: sometimes the goddess or spirit won't get the message or will willfully ignore it in pursuit of you. Or, even better, you can firmly (but kindly) let them know that you're not interested.

If you are interested, you could ask for a specific sign that the goddess or spirit is actually trying to contact you.

If you are the one trying to make contact, it is generally good manners to try to make contact with the goddess or spirit much like when you are invited to someone's house for the first time. Pay them compliments, offer gifts (tealights, fresh water, incense, and flowers are just about universally well received), and be polite. Do this once a week for a month. After the second week, start asking for a small sign that they are interested in continuing the conversation.

If they are not that into you, you'll know because either you will be the recipient of some ill fortune or, more likely, nothing will happen. All your little niceties will amount to a dead, wet, cold fish on the floor. Jesus is tasked to love all of our sad, sorry little selves; the rest of the spirits and goddesses are not.

You Received a Positive Omen! What Next?

Well, what kind of relationship do you want to have with this spirit or goddess? What kind of relationship do they appear to want to have with you? Do both visions match up? If you want to be equals and pals and she wants you to be a devotee with strict devotee boundaries, that may not be a great fit. How deeply involved do you want to get? Do you want your Witchcraft to be centered around this relationship, or do you want your craft to be something that you do and your goddess or spirit occasionally steps in to lend a hand with?

Don't Give In to Spiritual NRE (New Relationship Energy)

You know how, when you first start dating someone, you want to spend every minute of every day with that person and you would promise them anything? You know how you think that person is the

smartest, best-looking, funnest person alive? Then three months later you realize you have nothing in common, and you now think this person is vain, shallow, and stupid and you want nothing to do with them? Well, that experience isn't limited to the physical world. Sometimes initially you "click" with a goddess or spirit and you make vows, but then in a few months you don't want to keep them.

The problem is, generally speaking, goddesses and spirits have access to energy that you don't have access to. That's part of why you decided to work with goddesses and spirits. It can be a really good reciprocal relationship, but if one of you no longer wishes to reciprocate, then it can be a problem. Imagine working in a company of ten people and you start dating your boss. You dump your boss after promising that you would be together forever and spend every Sunday at their beach house for the rest of your lives. Your boss didn't want to break up, and jobs at other companies in your field are few and far between, so now you're stuck at this company. How do you suppose the next few years at work are going to play out? Not well.

So don't make any crazy vows or promises at the beginning of your new (spiritual) relationship unless you are willing to accept the consequences of your actions. Do something super crazy instead: get to know each other, keep giving offerings, get yourself attuned to their energy, and see if you're a good fit for each other.

Start as a Bottom Feeder

One of my mentors refers to herself as a "spiritual bottom feeder," meaning that for her, the relationship needs to be reciprocal—a favor for a favor. Start with small favors. Favors I've asked for include getting rid of a cold, a long nap, an evening that goes smoothly, etc. I do *X* (prayer, offerings, etc.) and ask for *Y*. If you try this a few times and it doesn't work, there's something wrong with the connection: that goddess or spirit is not interested in you, you're too grabby, they don't want to grant your requests for whatever reason, and so on.

Goddesses and spirits aren't magical gumball machines. If you're always going to them with your hands out, they're going to get annoyed with you. You need to build an actual connection between the two of you, ideally one that isn't built solely on the granting of favors. Think about it this way: If you ask a bunch of strangers for ten dollars, one of them might give it to you, but probably not. If you ask a friend for ten dollars, they will probably give it to you. On the other hand, if you're always asking that friend for a ten spot, they are going to feel used and abused and either cut you off as a friend or cut off the money.

But friends and family do often want to help you, especially if you've helped them in the past. The same is true of goddesses and spirits. If you are asking for a larger petition, you need to be willing to give more yourself—more time, better jewels, more energy, more devotion, or whatever your goddess or spirit is into. Typically, when asking, you would give the goddess or spirit half up front and the other half when your petition is granted.

But remember, goddesses and spirits can be just as opportunistic as any human (if not more so!). If you give a mouse a cookie, he'll probably want a glass of milk. In other words, if you're going to keep giving and giving and giving and not ask for anything back in the relationship, that goddess or spirit is going to ride you like a prize-winning show pony until you have nothing left. If that's not your goal, then you need to set some boundaries and the expectation of reciprocity. If that goddess or spirit is not willing to work within your boundaries, you need to do some serious thinking about whether you want to be in the relationship anymore. If you don't, you may need to consult someone, such as a mentor or a goddess or spirit you already work with, about how to extricate yourself from the situation.

Stranger Danger

For some reason, when dealing with goddesses and spirits, some people completely disengage from their common sense. After all, speaking with someone from the spirit world isn't common, so common sense shouldn't apply, right? Wrong. Until you get to know your new goddess or spirit, your guard should be up as much as it would be with a new acquaintance. Once you get to know your goddess or spirit better, your guard should be up about as much as it would be with a close friend, a sibling, or your spouse. They most likely would never willingly hurt you, but there's always that chance that they will. If something seems off, don't rush into agreeing to a relationship. Meditate on why it feels off. Ask for clarification.

You don't need to be hostile, and you don't need to be magically armed to the teeth—unless you are using force in your invocation and compelling the spirit to be your friend. That's sort of like trying to make friends by drugging a stranger, wrapping her in a rug, and tossing her in the back of your windowless white van. BFFs, right?!

If you want to consort with spirits that are known to be more dangerous, hey, it's your party and you can cry if you want to. Personally, I don't consort with people who require me to have a gun in my purse in my regular life, and I don't have any desire to consort with goddesses and spirits that require me to do the same. Just remember, "dark" doesn't always equal "dangerous," and "well known and well liked" doesn't always equal "safe." Use your critical thinking skills, use your gift of fear, use your common sense. It's a wild ride, but that's why we're Witches, right?

Deborah Castellano *is a frequent contributor to occult/Pagan sources such as the Llewellyn annuals, PaganSquare, and* Witches & Pagans *magazine. She blogs at* Charmed, I'm Sure *(www.charmedfinishingschool.com). Deborah's book,* Glamour Magic: The Witchcraft Revolution to Get What You Want, *will be published by Llewellyn in the summer of 2017. She resides in* New Jersey *with her husband, Jow, and their cat. She has a terrible reality television habit she can't shake and likes* St. Germain *liqueur, record players, and typewriters. Visit her at www.deborahmcastellano.com.*

Illustrator: Bri Hermanson

Crystal Magic: Not-So-Common Calcite

Ember Grant

Extremely popular among collectors, calcite doesn't always get the attention it deserves on the metaphysical scene. But if you practice crystal magic, you need to have several pieces of calcite in your collection. Calcite is essential and practical; it's found nearly everywhere on Earth—and it's gorgeous.

Calcium. We've all heard of it. It's the most abundant mineral in the human body—stored in our bones, as you probably know, and essential for many bodily processes and functions. In geological terms, calcite is a mineral—the crystallized form of calcium carbonate

(there are other calcium carbonate minerals, such as aragonite); typically, the word *calcium* refers to the chemical element. The name *calcite* comes from the German *calcit*, which has origins in the Latin *clax* and the Greek word *chalix*, which means "lime." This is because limestone is a rock composed of calcite and aragonite (in addition to the skeletal fragments of marine organisms). In addition, marble also contains calcite.

As an introduction to calcite, first we'll explore some of the variety that makes this mineral so appealing. Calcite can form hundreds of different crystal shapes and can be found in over a thousand rock combinations. This is one reason that it's so popular with mineral collectors. Although calcite is colorless or white in its pure form, gorgeous colors occur when other minerals blend with it during formation. In fact, nearly every color is possible. It can even be fluorescent and phosphorescent. Banded varieties can be found and are sometimes sold incorrectly as "onyx." A more accurate name for this particular stone is "Mexican onyx" or "limestone onyx"—genuine onyx is quartz and is colored black or black and white, and is a bit more valuable.

In recent years, a type called honeycomb calcite has been mined in Utah. It's yellow to orange in color and displays veined patterns that often resemble a honeycomb. It has a translucent quality with a beautiful golden glow. It's also referred to as honeycomb or amber onyx (and a variety of similar names). It's a versatile stone that is being used in many decorative and creative ways, from jewelry to countertops. It makes especially lovely candleholders.

If you've ever visited a cave, you also know calcite as the main mineral in some truly breathtaking cave formations, such as stalactites and stalagmites. And then there's travertine—those amazing "flows" of stone called *travertine terraces* (limestone containing calcium carbonate) are found famously in Yellowstone National Park and other locations around the world. These are created by hot water rising through the limestone carrying the dissolved calcium carbonate. The carbon dioxide is released, the calcium deposits are left behind, and the stone "grows," like those cave formations, but above the earth instead of inside it. Travertine can also occur in other areas, and not just around hot springs.

One notable formation of calcite is called Iceland spar (also called optical calcite). This type is known for its feature of double refraction. When a transparent piece is placed over written text, for example, the image is doubled.

Additionally, Picasso stone, a type of marble with a "painted" appearance, is an excellent choice and is often carved into cabochons for jewelry. Marble carvings are an excellent and inexpensive way to add calcite to your collection.

On an industrial scale, the importance of calcite cannot be overstated. It's the base component of cement, and many other materials are made using calcite, including chalk, paint, fertilizers, rubber, and abrasive cleansers. Marble and travertine have both been used throughout history in buildings and sculptures.

But what makes this mineral truly remarkable is its function in the human body. Aside from calcium's role in our teeth and bones, did you know that calcite crystals control our balance? There are pebbles of calcium carbonate inside a fluid in the inner ear (and in all vertebrates, in fact); when we move our heads, these little crystals signal the brain and guide us, basically helping us sense the directions of up and down. The loosening of these stones is sometimes responsible for the condition of vertigo—feeling dizzy and lacking a sense of direction.

Another interesting aspect of calcium in the human body is its presence in the pineal gland. This tiny gland in the brain produces melatonin and is the only gland in the body that converts serotonin into melatonin. It has been discovered that, similar to the crystals in the inner ear, there are microcrystals in this gland that contain calcium, carbon, and oxygen. Many scientific studies are being conducted on this area of the brain and its response to electromagnetic energy. It is believed that these crystals have a type of piezoelectric effect similar to quartz.

And because it neutralizes acid, calcium is used in antacids to relieve heartburn and indigestion. All this should simply add to our appreciation of this wonderful mineral.

Metaphysical Properties of Calcite

So how can you use calcite in magic? Its metaphysical properties are as diverse as its other uses. Calcite has a trigonal structure (which is a subdivision of hexagonal). Metaphysically, this means it has balancing properties. Other general metaphysical properties of calcite include amplifying energy (especially white and red) and promoting comfort

and healing (blue). It's good for memory and educational pursuits, specifically when studying the arts and sciences (yellow is the best choice in this case), and it enhances one's appreciation of nature (green variety). Since Iceland spar has the special quality of double refraction, it's often used for issues of duality and double meanings—specifically to clarify communication or help see other perspectives.

Marble can add clarity to meditation practice and aid dream recall. It can guide you to a state of stability and serenity. Marble is also a good "common sense" stone; it offers balance and protection, especially concerning the home environment. Picasso stone is especially useful for those engaged in the creative arts.

Since calcite is found literally in a rainbow of colors, there's a corresponding shade to use for clearing and activating each of the chakras. Clear or white calcite is appropriate for all of them, but clear is especially good for the crown chakra. And because of calcium's association with bones, many metaphysical healers use it to facilitate the healing of bone disorders.

Since calcite is found literally in a rainbow of colors, there's a corresponding shade to use for clearing and activating each of the chakras. Clear or white calcite is appropriate for all of them, but clear is especially good for the crown chakra.

For your collection, try to obtain at least one piece of Iceland spar, a mass of white calcite (or crystal mass), at least one well-formed crystal (or cluster), and as many colors as you can—especially red or pink, blue, green, and yellow. This will cover a wide range of magical purposes. Whether rough pieces or tumbled, most calcite has a "soft" feeling—smooth to the touch, with a waxy, satiny quality.

Using Calcite in Crystal Magic

Here are some specific techniques for using calcite in your crystal magic practice.

Keep a piece of yellow calcite on your desk or other work space. I like to use honeycomb calcite for this. I have a piece cut into a candleholder, which highlights the golden glow. You can simply light a candle (or use battery or electric lights) behind a thin slice of the stone to create the same effect. The glow is warm and soothing. In fact, I also have a tealight candleholder carved from golden calcite, and it's an excellent choice for this purpose as well. Allow the light to be your inspiration and guide you in reaching your intellectual goals.

Try holding a piece of Iceland spar while you meditate on clarity and issues of communication. It can help you see both sides of an issue or understand how to navigate when you're receiving confusing or mixed signals.

I have two small marble spheres, one solid white and one black with white veins. The black-and-white one is surprisingly useful for scrying; I often use the white one on my altar to symbolize the full moon. These spheres also display a delightfully subtle shimmer in candlelight.

Like quartz, calcite is common and affordable. You can find masses and crystals at gem and mineral shows, often for very reasonable prices. Just this year, I obtained two very large garden stones with calcite crystals for around ten dollars each. Granted, these are somewhat rough pieces, but they are still beautiful. Even large, well-formed pieces with impressive crystals can be purchased for around twenty dollars or less, although, naturally, you can expect to pay more for particularly striking specimens.

. . . .

Calcite is a stone that can help us foster a sense of community with those around us and with our world. We have it in our bodies; it's found in nature. We are intimately connected with the universe, and calcite can help remind us of that.

Sources

Aubrey, Allison. "Inner Ear 'Rock Slides' Lead to Vertigo." National Public Radio (April 27, 2009). www.npr.org/templates/story/story.php?storyId=103463398.

"Crystals of Your Body." Crystales. https://cristales.fundaciondescubre.es/?page_id=2151.

Edwards, Debbie. "The Piezoelectric Effect and the Pineal Gland in the Human Brain." Knoji (Jan. 10, 2012). https://physics.knoji.com/the-piezoelectric-effect-and-the-pineal-gland-in-the-human-brain.

Additional Information About Calcite

Galleries.com (Amethyst Galleries)

Geology.com

Minerals.net

Ember Grant *has been writing for the Llewellyn annuals since 2003 and is the author of three books and more than fifty articles. Her most recent book is* The Second Book of Crystal Spells. *She also sells handmade crafts and enjoys nature photography. Visit her online at* EmberGrant.com.

Illustrator: Kathleen Edwards

The Magick of Color

Najah Lightfoot

Long ago when the earth was new, massive ferns and wild palm fronds grew in abundance. All was green and misty. Young plants struggled to survive and gain a foothold in the tumultuous atmosphere.

There was little variation among the green beings. The process of photosynthesis was still evolving. Even the trees, which covered the planet, were nothing like the trees we have today. The trees in ancient days resembled something from a Dr. Seuss book. The world was covered in the muted colors of green and brown.

But one miraculous day, change came upon the planet. The first flowering plant arrived. Can you imagine the excitement and curiosity over the first flower? Homo sapiens weren't around to experience it, but you can be sure that whatever walked the earth sought out the flower's essence and magnificence. And when human beings found color, we began to create dyes made of natural fibers and materials, to bring peace, comfort, and joy into our world.

Mother Nature has given us a natural system. She gave us the magickal way of color, a complete system encapsulating the mind, body, and spirit.

She gave us plants and flowers, grown in her soil, nourished by the sun, moon, wind, stars, and rain. We in turn take those plants and flowers and dry them, press them, and boil them to extract colors, hues, and vibrations. And with the advance of technology, we have learned to make synthetic colors in hues and tones more brilliant than those found in nature.

When I first sat down to write this article, it had been only a couple of days since our beloved dog passed away, and I found myself drawn to the soothing colors of purple and pink. Purple filled my soul with peace, and pink comforted me and held me in love. I wore pink in the form of rose pentagram earrings, whose swinging vibrations lifted my spirits. I wore purple and pink until my grief lifted.

A wise practitioner once told me, "You've got to put yourself in it," meaning that although we may choose to follow someone else's directions, our work isn't truly our own until we put our own spin on it. Then it becomes personal, powerful work. So even though charts, websites, astrologers, and well-meaning friends may suggest what colors are best for you or for a spell, you need to listen to your heart's guidance and use colors that best align with your spiritual vibration.

You can use color to lift your spirit, heal your heart, protect yourself, connect with your goals, and remember your dreams.

Working with Color

I like to think about colors we can't see. Is there some new color that exists? Might there be a periwinkle lavender blue or a green magenta orchid? What if you could create your own color? What would it look like? How would you use it?

Guidelines exist to help you begin using color. When you're just starting out, it takes a while to build confidence and trust your own intuition.

Most of us are aware of the following basic color correspondences:

Red: passion, love, sex

Pink: love in a non-romantic sense

Blue: healing, the color of water

Yellow: the color of the sun, energy, safe travel

White: all-purpose color, healing, Spirit

Black: banishment, the void, power

Green: prosperity, spring, money, new growth

Purple: majesty, higher power

Brown: earth, grounding

Coloring books for adults are now all the rage, but some of us never left the crayon box behind. A lot of us have been coloring for ages. Perhaps you're a colorist, too. Take your love of color and let it embrace you, fill you up.

Each season brings its own tones and shades. Spring brings the vibrant chartreuse of new growth. Hyacinths pop with lavender purples, and daffodils bring the pale yellow of new beginnings.

Summer arrives with the lush shades of green. Flowers explode with vibrant reds and pinks. The sky is a gorgeous blue, while the sun is at its highest point, burning brightly with the golden yellow of starlight.

Fall arrives and the light begins to soften, taking on an otherworldly color. Fall leaves are at their most brilliant, bathing us in the colors of red, yellow, and gold and making us nostalgic for days gone by. Fall makes way for the quiet of winter. Reflection time is approaching.

Winter arrives (for some of us) and it seems the world is devoid of color. Stark tree branches stand as sentinels against the cold. A quiet blanket of snow covers the earth, yet prisms of color can be seen shining in ice crystals, which cover the land. Starved for color and light, we decorate our homes with garlands and twinkles and anything else that brings the promise of brighter days. Is this not why we celebrate the winter solstice and the winter holidays with such enthusiasm? We long for the promise of lighter, warm days. We anxiously await the return of color to boost and uplift us.

Perhaps color isn't something you use regularly. Personally I adore glitter. The sparkles of glitter make me happy. I like to say, "A day without glitter is like a day without sunshine." I use glitter sparingly in my eye shadows and lipstick, unless I'm attending a Pagan festival—then it's no holds barred!

Let's not forget about the myriad of colors in crystals. Crystals speak to our inner self and our intuition. Who hasn't had the wonderful

experience of going to a spiritual supply store and being drawn to a certain crystal? Oftentimes you have no idea why a certain crystal calls to you, yet you must have it. Energetically your vibration and the vibration of the crystal have aligned, making a match. You have found comfort in the crystal, and it too has aligned with you.

On an annual basis, Pantone.com announces the color of the year. The 2017 Pantone color of the year was Greenery, a color of new beginnings. Color is such an important factor in our lives that Pantone devotes an entire website to its color of the year. People use Pantone's information to design fabrics, create paint, and decorate the interior of their homes.

Colors of Emotion

There are also times when bright colors won't provide the comfort we seek. Traditionally people wear the color black for mourning. Why? Black is the color of sadness, of the unknown. But black can also be a color of power and honor. Who says you have to wear all black during times of grief? Maybe you're the one who shows up to the funeral in black with a flash of magenta to show death is not the end. In some cultures, grieving times are observed by wearing the color white.

Springtime in the Hindu religion brings one of the most vibrant expressions of color in the world. During the color festival of Holi, people participate in the ritual of throwing colored powders and waters. Originally the Holi festival was celebrated by married women. They threw colors to welcome spring and the full moon and to bring renewed life and compassion to their families. Today, revelers from Spain to New Delhi take part in the tradition of throwing vibrant colors of magenta, burnt orange, indigo, and golden yellow upon anyone who happens to cross their path on Holi Day. Googling "Holi Festival" will lift your spirits as you enjoy videos of people dousing each other with colored powders and waters, laughing and feeling the joy that color brings.

There are also YouTube videos on how to create your own Holi powders using natural plant and vegetable dyes. Just imagine the fun you could have holding your own Holi ritual. Wouldn't it be a blast to invite friends over during spring to make powders to use in ritual?

Of course in India it's much warmer in March than in some climates in the United States. If it's not possible to throw colors outside where you live, you could find a suitable indoor spot. The Holi Festival seems like a wonderful way to expand our Ostara rituals. Instead of dyeing eggs, make colored powders and throw them at your friends!

The use of color is also a science in the healthcare industry. The muted colors you see in hospitals and emergency rooms are there specifically to help calm and neutralize emotions. Hospitals are very emotional places, and much attention is paid to the use of color. It's pretty obvious why the color red would never be found there.

Color has also been used to intimidate or strike fear in people. People in authority may wear all black. Certain radical groups align with specific colors and symbols. Just as we can use magick for good or evil, color can be used to incite malevolent intentions. If certain colors cause ill effects in your being, stay away from them.

Your intuitive self knows which colors align with your spirit. By the same token, you may find that as you age, your color preferences change. That's okay too. We are all works in progress. Colors that may have suited you at one time in your life may no longer work for you in a different stage of life. If you never liked red but now find that red makes you feel hot and sexy, go for it!

• • • • • • • • • • • • •

Nature has given us the magick of color. We can use it to comfort, uplift, and heal. Allow color to take you where you've never gone before. Be bold! Be brash! Add a splash of color to your altar, your rituals, and your wardrobe. The results may surprise you.

Najah Lightfoot *is a freelance writer and a happy contributing author to the Llewellyn annuals. She is a priestess of the Divine Feminine, a martial artist, and an active member of the Denver Pagan community. She keeps her magick strong through the practice of Hoodoo, Pagan rituals, and her belief in the mysteries of the universe. She finds inspiration in movies, music, and the blue skies of Colorado. Find her online at www.twitter.com/NajahLightfoot, www.facebook.com/NajahLightfoot, and www.craftandconjure.com.*

Illustrator: Tim Foley

Magical Transformations

Everything Old Is New Again

Clean Eating for the Magical Practitioner

Tess Whitehurst

So many of us love working magic with plant ingredients that are as fresh and unprocessed as possible: grated ginger root, a clove of garlic, an acorn, a single red rose. And if they're locally grown or gathered, or we grew them ourselves, even better! Why? Because we know that nature is the source of our power, and that these pristine botanicals will not fail to enhance our magic with their potent energy and living presence.

But as every wise practitioner knows, magic does not begin and end with our spells and rituals. Rather, all of life is magical, and there is not a single second or activity that cannot be enhanced by a magical mindset. When you really think about it, could there possibly be a more magical activity than eating? As we know from the Charge of the Goddess, all acts of pleasure are rituals of the Goddess. And when we eat, not only are we engaging all our senses in a most pleasurable way, but we are also nourishing our bodies with precious fuel for life. We are partaking of the very earth herself, and our bodies are going about the very intricate and miraculous business of assimilating the earth's bounty in order to sustain our very selves: our skin, muscles, brain tissue, and bones.

On an energetic level, consuming living plants grown in the very body of Gaia is a way of receiving vibrational earth and plant wisdom straight from the planet and plants themselves. Like homeopathy, it's a way of bringing the healing vibration within us, and letting it permeate and transform our personal energy field from the inside out.

On an energetic level, consuming living plants grown in the very body of Gaia is a way of receiving vibrational earth and plant wisdom straight from the planet and plants themselves.

For example, imagine you're meditating outside on a beautiful day and then you mindfully eat a sweet, locally gathered apple or some strawberries from your garden. Notice how nourished you feel on every level. Now imagine that instead of the apple or strawberries, you eat a bag of cheese puffs or a hot dog. Notice the vast energetic difference: there's a closing down rather than an opening as your formerly highly vibrating body and energy field struggle to assimilate this stagnant and chemical-laden material.

Clean Eating: What It Is

While the term *clean eating* has been a buzzword for some time, there are a lot of differing definitions of the practice. For me and many others, clean eating simply means eating whole, plant-based foods and nothing else: whole fruits, vegetables, herbs, nuts, seeds, beans, and grains.

The benefits of eating this way are enormous. In addition to the considerable magical and energetic benefits just discussed, a whole plant food diet is an excellent way to open up your third eye and maximize your sensitivity to the energetic realm. On the physical level, clean eating supports a healthy body weight, radiant skin, vibrant energy, a clear mind, bright eyes, excellent digestion, and a consistently good night's sleep. It's also one of the very best ways to protect against cancer, diabetes, heart disease, and other debilitating illnesses.

On the macrocosmic level, no eating strategy supports our beloved planet more than plant-based, clean eating. Animal agriculture is by far one of the biggest threats to our water supply, which I'm sure you're aware is no small concern at this stage in the planet's history. And every time food is processed, packaged, or transported, it contributes to our planet's ecological decline. This means that the more natural, local, plant-based, and organic we eat, the better it is for Mother Earth, whom we as Witches adore and from whom we draw our power.

Then there is the level of your pocketbook. Clean eating employs such simple, single-ingredient foods—such as oats, brown rice, grapes, spinach, and olive oil—that you can literally find yourself saving hundreds of dollars in groceries per week. (Personally, my weekly grocery bill went down at least a hundred dollars when I made the switch, and I am only shopping for two!) And imagine all the medical bills you will avoid over the long haul by treating your body to such impeccable nutrition.

While at first eating only whole, plant-based foods might seem boring or bland, it doesn't have to mean eating nothing but celery and rice cakes. In fact, many delicious ingredients and condiments already fall under the clean-eating umbrella. For example, clean eating includes all of the following:

- Peanut butter and other nut butters
- Whole grain bread with olive oil
- Hummus with whole grain tortillas and lettuce
- Avocados (on anything)
- Popcorn with olive oil and salt
- Fresh fruit salad
- Unsweetened, whole grain cereal with almond milk, raisins, and cinnamon

- Fresh salad with oil, vinegar, and nuts
- Vegetable stir fry with rice and seasonings
- Grilled, baked, or scrambled tofu
- Whole grain pasta with tomato sauce
- Whole bean burritos with salsa and sautéed mushrooms
- Strawberries and unsweetened almond milk yogurt
- Fresh fruit smoothies with almond milk
- Unsweetened coffee or tea

Even if this sampling does initially strike you as bland, I have found that after a month or so of eating this way, your taste buds change. For example, a sugary treat is suddenly way *too* sugary, and you'd much prefer a bowl of fresh fruit salad anyway.

Making the Switch

Of course, if you're in the habit of eating meat, dairy, eggs, sugar, and/or processed foods, switching to clean eating will present some challenges. But once you make the switch, you will be so glad you did! Instead of craving sweetness and general satisfaction in life from your food, you'll begin to experience sweetness and a deep level of satisfaction from life itself. You'll feel alive and at home in your body, and people will begin to remark on your radiance. And you'll have plenty of energy for all the exciting and magical things you want to do! Plus, once you get over the initial cravings and withdrawals, it will feel easy and natural to continue with your positive new habit. (I promise!)

If you're already vegetarian or vegan, you can skip straight to full-fledged clean eating. But if you're eating meat, dairy, and/or eggs, you might want to begin with a meal plan that contains these things in smaller amounts. For a very reasonable price, you can purchase high-quality clean-eating meal plans of all three varieties (light meat with light dairy and eggs, vegetarian with light dairy and eggs, and full vegan) at www.fitnessblender.com. You might start with the meat-eating plan for a month and then move on to the vegetarian and follow up with the vegan. Alternatively, an excellent (and also reasonably priced) four-week plan for transitioning to a whole, plant-based diet can be found at forksoverknives.com.

To make the transition more fun, make a point of learning about the magical properties of the foods you're eating. Because when you eat clean, pretty much everything you eat is a magical ingredient that you're putting into the sacred medicine pouch that is your body. Luckily, there are a lot of great books on the subject, such as *Supermarket Magic* by Michael Furie, *The Supermarket Sorceress* by Lexa Roséan, and *Cunningham's Encyclopedia of Magical Herbs* by Scott Cunningham.

And, of course, let's not forget that you're magical, so you don't have to rely on willpower alone. Case in point: the following kitchen witchery spells.

I Am Nourished and Life Is Sweet: A Spell for a Successful and Smooth Transition to a Clean-Eating Diet

INGREDIENTS

- ½ cup unsweetened almond milk
- 1 cup rolled oats
- ⅓ cup raisins
- Cinnamon

On the first morning of your switch to a clean diet, assemble all the ingredients in one area on the kitchen counter. Ground and center yourself by taking three deep breaths and consciously connecting your energy with the core of the earth and the vast expanse of the cosmos. Hold your palms above the ingredients, and direct bright, golden white light and positive energy into them. Say:

By the powers of air and water, fire and earth,
I bless these foods, I praise their worth.
By the power of spirit and three times three,
Awaken their magic, so mote it be.

Heat the almond milk in a small pot until almost boiling, then add the oats and reduce the heat to a simmer. While occasionally stirring with a wooden spoon in a clockwise direction, chant or think, *I am nourished, I am nourished, I am nourished.* Continue until the oatmeal reaches the desired consistency. Transfer to a cereal bowl and add the raisins and a generous sprinkle of cinnamon. Stir in a clockwise direction with a cereal spoon while chanting or thinking, *Life is sweet, life is sweet, life is sweet.*

Before eating, hold the bowl in both hands and say:

I now commit to this transition to a clean-eating diet.
I dedicate my effort to Mother Earth.
May she support me in this effort and may we both be nourished,
balanced, and healthy,
Now and always.

Then, mindfully, eat.

Kitchen Blessing to Support Clean Eating

Once you begin your clean-eating adventure, your kitchen will become an alchemical laboratory of health, energy, well-being, and any other magical intention you want to work into your meals. But first, bless it as such.

Ingredients

- Natural cleaning supplies
- Geranium essential oil and an oil burner
- A chime or bell

Begin by pulling everything out of the freezer. Give it a good wipe, then put each item back in only if it's something that fits with your new eating style (or that your family will eat). Otherwise, compost, recycle, and/or give away the items as appropriate. Repeat with each shelf and drawer in the fridge and then with each cupboard. Follow up by cleaning the rest of the kitchen thoroughly.

When the kitchen is very clean, diffuse the geranium essential oil. Say:

Kitchen be magical, kitchen be blessed,
As I now prepare only Mother Earth's best.
Nourished and healthy, vibrant and strong,
May living foods nourish me (or us) all the year long.

Ring the bell or chime three times.

Sugar Withdrawal/Sugar Craving Combat Spell

The unfortunate truth is that if we're not eating clean, we're probably addicted to sugar, even if it's in the form of something as seemingly innocuous as agave nectar, honey, or fruit juice. (While clean eating does allow for whole fruit, which acts as a cleansing tonic for your digestive system, fruit juice behaves like a sugar in your body and is not recommended.) As such, when you switch to a whole-food, plant-based diet, you may encounter a serious sugar withdrawal.

And make no mistake: sugar withdrawals are serious. This is something I learned the hard way. Even though I thought my diet was relatively healthy, I experienced cravings, headaches, extremely low energy, and even nausea about a week or two into my clean-eating switch.

But like all withdrawals, they eventually pass when our bodies balance out. Until then, this spell will help.

Ingredient

- Your favorite fruit (or the fruit that sounds best to you right now)

Wash and prepare a bowl of your choice of fruit. Hold the bowl in both hands and say:

Mother Earth, I call on you.
Sweeten this moment, help me get through.
Balance my body, strengthen my soul,
With the magical sweetness contained in this bowl.

Envision golden white light entering and surrounding the fruit. Then, mindfully, eat.

Your Healthiest, Happiest Year Yet

You don't have to just wish for a healthy, happy year; you can make the switch to clean eating and proactively make it come true. Yes, it might take a little while to get out of the old habits and into the new ones, but it's so, so worth it. You'll say goodbye to cravings, food addiction, and sugar highs and lows while beginning to love the way your body looks and feels more than ever before ... all while getting more in tune with Mother Earth and all of the power and magic she has to offer!

Tess Whitehurst *is the author of* The Magic of Flowers Oracle *and a number of books about magical living, including* Magical Housekeeping *and* Holistic Energy Magic. *She's also the founder and facilitator of the Good Vibe Tribe, an online magical community and learning hub. Visit her at www.tesswhitehurst.com.*

Illustrator: Jennifer Hewitson

Staying on the Spiritual Wagon

Blake Octavian Blair

A lot of time, energy, dedication, and work is required to maintain a strong and healthy spiritual practice. However, what do we do when schedules crunch, mundane life happens, or crisis hits? It can be easy to feel like we've lost our way, like we've fallen off the proverbial spiritual wagon.

I understand this feeling. I (and many others, I assure you) have been through periods like that before. Don't fear—there are ways to get through it and maintain a connection with divinity and your spiritual practice. There are spiritual lifelines, so to speak, to help you stay afloat.

Join me as we look at ways to stay on the spiritual wagon and perhaps even strengthen our spiritual practice while doing so.

There are many situations in life that may lead us to feel as though there just isn't enough time for an involved spiritual practice, including employment uncertainty, having to move, the death of a loved one, having a baby, or dealing with conditions such as depression or anxiety. The stress and emotions felt during such periods of duress can seem paralyzing. However, allow me to gently suggest that it is worth finding ways to keep your spiritual luster, even if it feels like you're running on a spiritual emergency generator simply to keep going. After all, is that not one part of what spirituality is meant to be helpful for: to provide the means and wisdom to assist us in making our way through the rough times as well as the good? Magical people often pride themselves on the practicality and proactivity of their spiritual beliefs.

If you have never been in a situation that threatens to toss you from your spiritual wagon, then consider yourself lucky. The truth is that, at one time or another in life, we all will go through at least one rough patch. For example, if you have one employment situation come to an end, whether it's planned or unplanned, you may face the uncertainty of the job hunt. The job market today is not what it was in past generations. Finding the right employment situation under a strict deadline—and hoping it will take you to a place

If you have never been in a situation that threatens to toss you from your spiritual wagon, then consider yourself lucky. The truth is that, at one time or another in life, we all will go through at least one rough patch.

where you'll be happy living and provide the resources needed for you and your family to live comfortably—might be enough to occupy your mind, consume your energy, and throw you from your wagon.

Dealing with the unknown is scary. When my husband was finishing graduate school, we were looking at employment opportunities for him and where they would take us geographically. It was stressful, even with promising prospects on the horizon. It was certainly overwhelming, but we were able to stay on the spiritual wagon by allowing ourselves to acknowledge the situation directly in some of our spiritual work, in addition to giving ourselves some wiggle room in our spiritual practices, seeking counsel from friends and community members, and accepting healing from others.

As practitioners in the tradition of core shamanism, we consciously made the effort to maintain our shamanic journey practice, as it helped sustain us as we received wisdom and compassionate healing from our helping spirits on the situation. Further, we made regular offerings to the spirits for their assistance and prayers for what we wanted to unfold, leaving regular biodegradable offerings in a local body of water. These practices and ceremonies were manageable for us to maintain and allowed us some leeway schedule-wise, without the pressure of a strict regimen that was "do or fail." In this time of crisis, a requirement of doing a ritual at a very precise time in an ultra-precise way just wouldn't have been possible. However, we were able to maintain a spiritual connection, and it allowed our practice to help us through the rough patch.

We also sought the counsel of spiritual community members. We were lucky to have a few friends from one spiritual community we belonged to who had been through a similar situation and knew the ins and outs of the occupational field we were dealing with. Having a listening ear and their big-picture advice based on experience was extremely helpful, and they were very supportive throughout the process. We also accepted the help, advice, and spiritual work of colleagues in our shamanic, Pagan, and Reiki communities. For example, one particularly close friend sent us distance Reiki nightly, and I'm certain it contributed to helping us get where we needed and wanted to go. Sometimes we all need advice, healing, a listening ear, or just someone to take our mind off things for a little bit and make us smile or know we are loved. Those of you reading this who deal with depression and/or anxiety, or perhaps have a loved one who does, can testify to the value of that last piece of advice. Sometimes you just need to be able to call upon a friend who can simply be there for you. All the better if you share similar spiritual viewpoints and can offer support in that way as well.

When times get tough, it's often easier to engage in spiritual practices along with a friend or spiritual colleague. I have a close friend and shamanic sister who felt she had kind of lost her spiritual mojo after the birth of her two children and the death of her mother. Those three major life events all happened within the span of a few years. The energy, effort, and motivation she needed for her spiritual practice had up and left. Her connection to the divine felt neutral in strength at best. When she did have the get-up-and-go to do something, she often felt disconnected in her workings. What had not left and was not absent was desire. The desire for spiritual connection and power was present.

It was shortly after this friend gave birth to her second child that my husband and I met her and we became fast and close friends. She was very interested in our shamanic practice, and we gave her our teachers' information. She began studying with them, and through this new lens she found a fresh outlook on her spiritual practice that resonated and felt like home, and she quickly got her spiritual groove back. She found an outlet that resonated with her experiences, fit her life, and had a built-in community with friends that shared the tradition and new teachers to guide her, providing a spiritual support system.

The value of spiritual community is not to be underrated when you're going through a tough time, no matter what your particular beliefs are. It's not necessary to have an entire traditional church congregation, but having even a handful of friends with similar beliefs can go a long way. Whether they are local to you or available via phone or online, being part of a community is a huge asset.

Another excellent tool for spiritual engagement exemplified by my friend's story is taking a class or learning new skills. This can seem like a huge undertaking during times of stress, but if conditions allow for you to do so, it can be a great way to reenergize your spiritual batteries, build community, and gain resources to help you carry on. Taking a class related to your spiritual path can not only help take your mind off things for a little while, but can also give you tools to face your situation head-on and help you manifest and plan for a better outcome.

When tough times hit, a few things tend to happen straight away and then persist throughout the rough patch that make it feel difficult to stay the course in a spiritual practice. One is the experience of the "monkey mind." Generally the monkey mind takes the form of obsessive worry during times of crisis; the "what if" thought pattern kicks in. The other thing that tends to kick in is a feeling of being overwhelmed. You may feel like you don't have the time or the ability to take the time for your spiritual activities, or you may not feel sure that you can concentrate or give a hundred percent to them.

This is where flexibility can really come into play. Giving yourself flexibility and allowing for some simplification does not dilute the potency, meaning, or devotional expression of your spirituality. A handful of flower petals offered by saying a prayer and tossing them into a lake can be as meaningful as an elaborate, full-ritual offering ceremony done in a temple room before an altar in a cast circle. A simpler version is certainly easier to execute and fit into your schedule when you are under stress and have limited energy. I have also found, in my own times of crisis, that if I can get myself to engage in simple spiritual practices, it puts me in a better place to

Giving yourself flexibility and allowing for some simplification does not dilute the potency, meaning, or devotional expression of your spirituality. A handful of flower petals offered by saying a prayer and tossing them into a lake can be as meaningful as an elaborate, full-ritual offering ceremony done in a temple room before an altar in a cast circle.

engage in more vigorous or involved spiritual practices. You just have to find that starting point to center yourself, even just a bit. A further benefit I've noticed is that after I engage in a spiritual practice, my focus outside of my spiritual practice improves and I have greater clarity and feel a bit more calm. You may still be stressed, but perhaps a bit less so, and your coping ability may improve. Additionally, it is my personal experience that the divine realms will also come to your assistance, and that is a powerful benefit.

You can see that your spiritual practice can become part of your self-care. *Self-care* is quite the buzz term in holistic and alternative health circles these days. When I use the term, I am referring to the things you can do to maintain your own spirit. Perhaps this is simply giving yourself fifteen minutes of quiet time in the morning or at lunch every day. Maybe it's knitting or craft time. It could be a weekly candlelit bubble bath. It can be anything that rejuvenates you, feels restorative, and leads you to a place of calm. My mother-in-law, for example, enjoys yoga, and it fulfills these goals for her. Personally, I find chocolate is a great addition! Whatever you choose, make self-care a priority, be flexible, and find something that fits into your life, but make your spiritual practice a part of it.

With all of my talk of having a spiritual support system and being able to have a phone-a-friend type of spiritual lifeline available, I want to give a little attention to the role of being a supportive friend. I'm sure most folks reading this are the type of person who would want to be there for a loved one going through such a life event. As I mentioned, the majority of us have been through rough patches. We can often speak from experience and perhaps be a beacon of light in the dark tunnel our friend may be traveling through. I once heard a friend, who is a Unitarian Universalist minister, say in a sermon, "If you're going through hell, keep driving!" However, sometimes that takes encouragement, and it's nice to have a sane passenger or friend

to provide a rest stop to show us there is good outside the rough patch. It is important, however, not to speak outside your experience. If you don't truly understand the person's situation, do not—I repeat—do NOT say to them "I understand." If you can't back up that statement, it will fall flat and ring hollow. It's better just to be a voice of compassion and provide a listening ear. Sharing a relevant personal experience and your understanding can be wonderful, but the last thing a person in crisis wants is empty reassurance.

Above all, be genuine. Sometimes when you are helping a friend through a crisis, it is worth acknowledging that it is okay to feel down, upset, nervous, worried, or any number of other emotions. However, it's good to remind your friend that those feelings don't have to be all-consuming and then try to provide them with a little relief and perhaps hope with your company. When going through a rough patch, it can be a wonderful thing to get a random phone call or message from a loved one who is just checking in on us. There can be light at the end of the tunnel, even if we don't yet see it... it may be just around the corner. While it may not seem like it at the time, the crisis is likely not the end game.

Certainly you can be proactive beyond providing a listening ear, often by helping your friend through spiritual practice. If you share similar beliefs, this may take the form of co-practice. Perhaps perform some proactive magick together to address the situation. Magick combined with real-world action has a pretty good track record of having a degree of success. Most practitioners would testify to that. Of course, you can also engage in magick and ritual for reasons that help give a person's mind a rest from thinking about the situation and a chance to refresh. Perhaps plan a simple sabbat celebration together. It can be helpful to be reminded that, despite the rough times, the Wheel of the Year still turns and Mother Nature is still ever present for us. The Great Mother watches over us all.

It is also possible that your loved one does not share your style of spiritual practice and, in fact, may not even be of a magickal persuasion. However, with their permission, you can still help them through your own spiritual practice. Permission is paramount and just plain shows respect. How many times have you been annoyed by people who don't agree with your beliefs passively-aggressively saying, "I'll pray for you." Let's avoid any chance of that. However, most people are incredibly open-minded. I accept prayers from well-intentioned and open-minded friends and family who are of different faiths, and I find most people are similarly open. So light a candle for a friend, send them Reiki, or do shamanic healing work for them with your spirits' assistance. Further, encourage them to continue some simple spiritual practice of their own, even if it's a different path from yours. You don't have to be of their faith to be supportive of it.

We can hope for ourselves and others that we will never experience a time when we feel depression, despair, or deep worry over how our lives are working out. The reality, however, is that most of us will go through a rough patch here and there. We can be there for each other. The truth is, the vast majority of the time, things can and do work out. What the scenery looks like after we exit into the light at the end of the tunnel may be vastly different than what we envisioned, but most of the time things turn out just fine. In fact, I think the spiritual work my husband and I did during our rough patches certainly contributed to manifesting good outcomes for us.

As you navigate challenging situations and work toward solutions, remember the various techniques we discussed. Try to maintain a simple spiritual practice, be gentle on yourself, and allow for flexibility! Spend time with supportive people. Seek the counsel of your spiritual support system, in this "ordinary" realm and in the realms of the spirits and gods. It is my sincere hope that with some of the tips presented here, you can not only stay on your spiritual wagon but ride it through the tough times. Blessed be!

Blake Octavian Blair *is an eclectic Pagan, ordained minister, shamanic practitioner, writer, Usui Reiki Master-Teacher, tarot reader, and musical artist. Blake blends various mystical traditions from both the East and West along with a reverence for the natural world into his own brand of modern Paganism and magick. Blake holds a degree in English and Religion from the University of Florida. He is an avid reader, knitter, crafter, and practicing pescatarian. He loves communing with nature and exploring its beauty, whether within the city or while hiking in the woods. Blake lives in the New England region of the USA with his beloved husband. Visit him on the web at www.blakeoctavianblair.com or write him at blake@blakeoctavianblair.com.*

Illustrator: Rik Olson

Boundaries and Cleanup for Magickal Events

Emily Carlin

One of the most rewarding elements of magickal community is participating in community events such as group rituals, study groups, and festivals. They allow us to share energies, build friendships, exchange knowledge, support one another, and have a great time while doing so. There is no better way to support and strengthen your local community than by hosting an event, be it something as small as a study group in your home or as large as a public festival. Beyond mundane considerations, hosting a magickal event requires consideration of the potential energies of attendees and the consequences the meeting of those energies can generate. Let's discuss some of the energetic concerns, protective preparations, and energetic cleanup techniques for magickal events.

Energetic Concerns

To say that magickal people have unique energies would be a profound understatement. Any time people get together in a group, you're always going to have a unique mix of energies; gather magickal folk en masse and you'll soon find yourself swimming in a unique gumbo of energetic overflow, sparking emotions, and colliding shields of varying levels of effectiveness. Magickal people tend to have very strong personal energies, because we are more mindful of them and work to make them more potent in the world. Consequently, a magickal person having a bad day or with cracked shields or negative intentions is likely to have

a greater effect on others than a non-magickal person. Not all practitioners, be they new or veteran, have their own energies under conscious control, and certainly not at all times. Whether they mean to or not, magickal people can be incredibly disruptive to those around them if their energies are in conflict.

Magickal folks also potentially bring unacknowledged metaphysical guests with them. Practice magick for a while and sooner or later you will become acquainted with unseen entities such as spirits, faeries, deities, ancestors, angels, demons, etc. Unseen entities tend to congregate around magickal people, and they will follow those people to your event. Not all of these unseen entities are positive and not all of them get along with one another. Host enough events and eventually you may have to deal with someone's unwanted passenger deciding that someone else at the event looks tastier than their current host and then trying to follow the new person home. As a host, you have a certain level of responsibility for the energetic safety of your invitees and must do what you reasonably can to prevent such problems.

Practice magick for a while and sooner or later you will become acquainted with unseen entities such as spirits, faeries, deities, ancestors, angels, demons, etc. Unseen entities tend to congregate around magickal people, and they will follow those people to your event. Not all of these unseen entities are positive.

Pre-Event Magick

Before hosting a magickal event, it is important to set a specific intention for the event and place formal wards. Doing so will help the energies of the event run smoothly.

Intention Setting

A formal intention setting is a small ritual that sets an energetic anchor for your event. This ritual should be performed by the event organizers prior to the arrival of the first invitee. Depending on the size and scope of your event, you may choose to do this the day of the event or many months in advance.

In this ritual, you would call on any patron entities or metaphysical allies the event might have and request that they watch over and protect it. This would also be an appropriate time to communicate with the local spirits of the land and ask their permission to hold the event. Then read a formal statement of your short- and long-term goals for the event, the energies you hope the event will create and maintain, and whom you want in attendance. If there are particular people or entities you do not want to attend your event, you may add a prohibition at this time.

After clearly stating your intent, it is important to declare your event as energetic safe space. As mentioned earlier, your guests will bring their own energies, alignments, and metaphysical friends with them. Set your event as safe space for all of your invitees and demand that they play nicely with each other during the event. Strong communication and directly addressing conflicts are necessary for the health of any community; needless bickering and energetic backbiting are not. Clearly state the consequences for violating this safe space, both for unseen entities and people, and make sure they are widely known. By firmly establishing your intent and boundaries, you will set the energy for the entirety of your event.

Wards

Apart from the standard shields one would normally set for any magickal working, I recommend laying down a series of warding jars both to protect your event and to normalize potentially hazardous energy spikes. Acquire several small jars, about one cup to one pint in size. Fill the jars halfway with salt. I prefer to use either black salt or Epsom salt. Then add a good pinch each of baking powder, cascarilla powder, red brick dust, mugwort, rosemary, and lavender.

Set a jar in each major space used by the event. The contents will absorb and neutralize negativity as well as excess energy throughout the event. If your event lasts for several days, you may need to refresh the ingredients in the jars periodically, depending on the energies floating about. After the event, the contents of the jars should be either buried or thoroughly cleansed in moonlight and thrown away. Note that salt can be toxic to plants in large amounts, so be mindful of where you dispose of it.

Post-Event Cleanup

Any gathering of magickal people will inevitably stir up the energies of the space they've inhabited, and it is the duty of the event organizers to soothe those energies back to their natural state. Simply leaving a surfeit of non-naturalized energy in a given space can be as useless as piling a ton of fertilizer in one square foot of space or as potentially destructive as chumming shark-infested waters.

How far you should take your energetic cleanup depends on both the nature of the energy you find yourself left with and the intrinsic energies of the space. If you have little leftover energy or it's similar to the energy of the place, then a simple but deliberate grounding into the natural environment should suffice. Even then, be mindful to ground thoroughly so as not to attract unwanted metaphysical attention to the space that has hosted you. If the energy clashes with the natural space, then you should direct it to ground in a space more aligned with its nature. For example, if you find yourself with the energy of wild and uncontrolled nature in the middle of an office complex, you may wish to move that energy out into a local forest or nature preserve before grounding it. Direct your cleanup in a way that is mindful of the space.

Whether the space is public or private should also be taken into consideration. Private spaces, like someone's home or a small business, have particular energies, and you should do your best to restore the energies to their state prior to the event. Public spaces, like parks and hotels, have a more neutral energy and thus can be cleansed more generically. High-traffic public spaces are also less likely to hold on to the energies raised by your event. While that doesn't mean you should be lackadaisical in your efforts, it does mean you needn't worry quite as much about getting things back to square one.

Once you've cleansed the space to your satisfaction, you should make an offering of gratitude. Giving thanks both to the spirits of the place and to the people who provided/worked the space is an important capstone for your event. Making an offering to the spirits of the place that hosted you and any entities that aided in the success of your event both cultivates a healthy relationship with them and ends your event with positivity. Besides simply being good manners, an explicit thanks to the people who hosted you cultivates your good name and helps the reputation of your entire community.

A good event organizer has a responsibility both to their invitees and to the space hosting the event to safeguard them from negative or harmful, disruptive energies. Taking the time and effort to identify potential energetic concerns, set up boundaries beforehand and enforce them, and properly clean up afterward can make all the difference in the success of an event while it's happening as well as its long-term impact. Such simple steps show awareness of and respect for the myriad energies that dance together at any magickal gathering and strengthen the whole community.

Emily Carlin *is an eclectic Witch, writer, teacher, mediator, and ritual presenter based in Seattle. She currently teaches one-on-one online and at in-person events on the West Coast. For more information and links to her blogs, go to http://about.me/ecarlin.*

Illustrator: Kathleen Edwards

My Mother's Funeral: Bringing Pagan Ritual into Death

Jane Meredith

My mother died while I was in Paris. She was in her early seventies and had been unwell for several years, occasionally quite ill but never actually dying. A few days before her death she was at her retirement party, celebrating her contribution to an organization in which she had played a fundamental role. She had given a speech and been walking around, drinking champagne, talking and laughing with people. It was a sudden death and, I think, not a bad one. But still a death.

The requirements of handling a death in the family kicked in. The fact that I was completely dazed and in shock did not seem to stop me from rebooking a flight, canceling workshops and events, and talking to various people on the phone. There was to be a funeral, which had to be planned. I said, on the phone, *I'll do it.* And in their state of shock and disarray, no one contradicted me or tried to talk me out of it.

I'm a Pagan, a magical practitioner, a Goddess worshipper. Ceremonies and rituals are what I excel at. I've run hundreds of them and attended probably hundreds more. I did not have a moment's doubt that planning my mother's funeral was something I could do. I understand the structures of ritual. And about fifteen years earlier, my mother, my son Damon (then six), and I had run my grandmother's funeral; I remember how impressed the minister celebrant had been with us. This time there would be no celebrant other than myself and Damon, now twenty-two.

I'm a Pagan, a magical practitioner, a Goddess worshipper. Ceremonies and rituals are what I excel at. I've run hundreds of them and attended probably hundreds more. I did not have a moment's doubt that planning my mother's funeral was something I could do.

He flew from Sydney to Melbourne to be with my father, while I negotiated the much longer flights involved from Paris to Melbourne. The celebration of my mother's life fell together like the best rituals do. The jigsaw pieces of it chunked together in my mind. At the time it seemed of the utmost importance that this be done as perfectly as possible, that it be fitting for her, that this ritual be an offering to her life. At my parents' house, I talked through the ritual with my son: the format, the content, the timing. He said, "This is going to be great!"

I was raised with no religion, which is not uncommon in Australia. The fact that I became religious, follow a spiritual path, and even write about it and perform it publicly is never mentioned by my family. Occasionally, if I happen to mention something connected with it, the comment is politely side-stepped. So the funeral would not be a Pagan ritual (although perhaps all funerals are Pagan rituals), but it would be a well-constructed, participative, celebratory ritual. The ceremony had been scheduled (while I was still on a plane and had no say in it) for the exact day of Imbolc in Australia, on August 2.

My mother was a gregarious person, with a large presence, personality, and involvement in the world. She had not gone through years of gradual removal from the interactions of life that some drawn-out dyings impose; there were literally hundreds of people touched by and shocked by her death, and over a hundred of them planned to attend this celebration. Many of them had been talking with her or had seen her just a few days before. Occasionally, while listening to my plans, one person or another expressed doubt: *Will that really work? What if nothing happens? How will you be able to do that?* And each time, simply from my experience in rituals over the years, I knew it would work. I know how people behave in ritual, I understand the way to offer invitations that will be accepted, I trust my leadership in it, and I have a working ritual relationship with Damon.

Although the funeral company insisted that they were completely happy to hand the ceremony over to us, they must have been employing some kind of placating-the-grieving methodology, because at every turn they suggested substitutes for what I had planned. The thing that upset them the most was my idea to have three men and three women as coffin bearers. They argued against it repeatedly, citing height differences, unfamiliarity of the carriers with this task, and the relative ease of handing the task over to them, all of which I disregarded. I warned my brother (who is capable of acerbic dismissal) to be on guard against this, as each time we had to move the coffin—from the hearse into the hall, back out again, and then from the hearse to the gravesite—they stepped forward, miraculously ready, and suggested that they do it instead of our motley assortment of carriers, who ranged from a tall twenty-year-old boy who'd known my mother all his life, to a woman friend of my mother's, surely also in her seventies, to a middle-aged niece and my aged-but-fit father.

One of my mother's eccentricities was a devotion to stuffed toys, partly in line with her passion for children's literature, so her toys included small but perfect versions of the Wild Things, a Piglet and an Eeyore, a puffin from Puffin books, and many others. In my own collection I have a baby pink flamingo soft toy from her, and my son has a Peter Rabbit. I thought it would be fitting—and that it would lighten both the mood and the setting of somber wood, stone, and small diamond-paned windows—if people brought stuffed toys with them. So we put it on the invitation. Many reservations were expressed to me about the wisdom of this, the likelihood of it occurring, and people's possible disdain for the idea. But those coming knew my mother. They brought soft toys—most people brought one and some brought several. They put them on the heavy wood slab tables that filled the hall, and sat on the benches on either side of them. From the slightly raised stage, looking down, I saw a hall filled with people and bears, pandas, dolls, giraffes, octopuses, mice, dolphins, and many other kinds of animals. My own loyal zebra, who'd been in Paris with me, was there.

The ceremony was held in a medieval-style banquet hall, just up the road from where my parents lived, part of an artists' community adjoining the local cemetery. My brother and I had played there as children; I had attended drama workshops, poetry conferences, and a wedding in this hall and spent countless childhood hours wandering the grounds.

We began with a poem that I recited at my father's request, and then it was time for the speeches. Damon, the final speaker, stood up and said, "In the religion in which I was raised, today is a special day. We call it Imbolc." He spoke about spring bulbs, which my mother had loved, and about the earth awakening, and he said, "Maybe death is a different kind of awakening." He taught us a song, a Pagan chant, but no one really needed to know that and everyone sang.

Then we launched into the most controversial part of the program. We had left half an hour for people to get up and share a memory of my mother. I asked for thirty people to get up and speak for a minute each. This was not rehearsed, and we had not preselected any except for the first two speakers. My father doubted that anyone would get up, but Damon and I knew they would. Damon worked the floor, walking around and asking people if they like to go up and speak, while I organized those waiting for their turn. Someone sat in the audience with a watch and timed the speakers, ready to signal to me if someone went over a minute, but amazingly no one did.

We heard how my mother had influenced a young woman who was in the same profession, and we laughed at many funny stories, such as the time my mother had suggested to a colleague, when they were stuck in an overheating car, that he take the frozen peas he'd just bought and put them on the car engine. School friends, colleagues, friends, neighbors, and relatives all shared their stories, small pieces of my mother's life coming together to commemorate her.

Then we moved the coffin the few hundred meters from the hall to the grave that had been prepared, and I spoke a Native American prayer that had been over Damon's bed when he was small. Next, Damon read aloud two bedtime stories, one he had written himself and *Where the Wild Things Are*. He let that book fall into the grave, onto her coffin. We had native flowers and let people pick one and drop them in with a blessing. Our ritual was complete, from the invocation of the poem to the conclusion of a story, flowers, and blessings. The plaque there now bears a line from the *Wild Things*: "Let the wild rumpus begin."

So many people came up to me after the service. They said, incredulously, that it was the best funeral they had ever attended. They said they loved it, looking askance as they said it; it's not what you usually say at funerals. They asked me to run their own funeral. They said it was so like my mother. And they asked me, again and again, how I was able to do it: stay so calm and manage to hold everything together.

And yet for me it was natural. Not instinctive—I mean, it was my training. I joked (maybe especially to myself) that it was the only way I could ever get my mother to a ritual of mine. That at last I had been able to contribute something meaningful to her. That for once my skills had met her requirements. Pagan rituals are not done without emotion, without feeling; they come out of great depth of connection to the earth and our lives and the lives of those around us. They are built on that. It wasn't that I was calm exactly, but that I was using my skills in a profoundly meaningful way and my emotion fed into the focus of that.

I believe that we—Pagans, ritualists, Witches, magicians—have an enormous gift to offer our non-Pagan communities and families: the ability to construct and run deeply personal and powerful rituals. The ceremonies do not have to be religious, though they may fit the requirements of a different religion, such as Buddhism, Christianity, or Judaism. When ceremonies are constructed and run by us, our grief will inform and charge the proceedings as we offer our skills and practice to our families and communities. We know what brings people into a ritual space and what leaves them cold or uninvolved. We know the components of a successful ritual and also how to rescue one that's failing. We know how to hold energy, and how to build it and release it. We understand and are in relationship with the unseen forces, from deities to land spirits to the dead themselves. We know how to walk with a foot in each world and how to work together in ritual.

I believe that we—Pagans, ritualists, Witches, magicians—have an enormous gift to offer our non-Pagan communities and families: the ability to construct and run deeply personal and powerful rituals.

Let's give these gifts—not just to those within our Pagan communities but also to those who might never know the ceremony they attended was drawn from Pagan practice.

Jane Meredith *is an Australian author and ritualist. Her latest book, co-authored with Gede Parma, is* Magic of the Iron Pentacle: Reclaiming Sex, Pride, Self, Power & Passion. *Her previous books include* Circle of Eight: Creating Magic for Your Place on Earth *and* Journey to the Dark Goddess. *Jane is passionate about mythology, magic, dark chocolate, rivers, and trees. She teaches in person as well as distance courses and also teaches in the* Reclaiming Tradition. *Her website is www.janemeredith.com.*

Illustrator: Tim Foley

Insect Totems: Creepy, Crawly, Buzzy Wisdom

Tiffany Lazic

Our spirits soar when guided by the majesty of the Eagle or Hawk totem, urging us to rise above mundane concerns or inviting us to draw upon the wisdom of ancestors. A deep heart connection and feelings of kinship often arise toward the animals that walk this land with us, such as bear, wolf, or stag. At times we may feel as though we ourselves are part of their tribe, pack, or clan. Even the creatures of the sea can call to us when we find ourselves out of our depths. In times of confrontation, these teachers offer a variety of responses, from the dolphin's intelligence and grace to the shark's stealth and fearlessness. To be sure, there are those creatures of sky, land, and sea that may make us twitchy, but on the whole, we tend to be able to see something somewhat familiar in them. We embrace them, meditate on them, and even tattoo them on our bodies. Even in those cases when we may feel fear when faced with a particularly harsh or stern animal teacher, we don't have a tendency to feel revulsion. That virulently strong emotion is most often reserved for the tiniest of teachers—those that have a greater chance of slipping past our gaze unnoticed. Ironically enough, it is these teachers that have been with us the longest and may have the most to teach us.

Insects have arguably been on earth longer than any other living creature. The American Association for the Advancement of Science suggests that insects have been around for 479 million years! Compared with dinosaurs, which roamed the earth from 65 to 230 million years ago, and modern humans, who are a mere 200,000 years young, insects helped to shape the world in which we live and created a precedent for activities that keep us alive, such as forming a social structure and farming.

Insects are the most species rich of all the earth's creatures, numbering about 900,000 different species. Given that they are so very small, and new species are being discovered all the time, conservative estimates of the true number of insect species, according to the Smithsonian Institute, put the number at closer to 30 million. Further astounding numbers place insect biomass at approximately 300 pounds of insect for every human pound. From a population perspective, the current estimate of the total global human population is 7.4 billion. A single locust swarm has been estimated at 1 billion. The insect world offers a massively diverse and rich variety of potential for totem medicine.

General Insect Medicine

When it comes to examples of how to thrive in society, there is almost no other area in nature that offers better guidance than the insect world. Bees, ants, wasps, and termites have developed highly evolved social structures that include division of labor, cooperative brood care, and contribution from all members. Additionally, insects are the superheroes of the natural world, demonstrating remarkable feats of strength and endurance. Spittlebugs can jump 100 times their own length, and fleas can jump 150 times their own height! All insects have the potential to teach us how to access untold reserves within ourselves, but each individual species also provides its own specific message and teaching.

Challenging Insects We Resist

As in so many areas in our lives, here too with the array of insect teachers and totems we find the dark cast of the Shadow. The Shadow consists of those aspects of the self that are rejected or repressed. Unconsciously we fear that what lives in our Shadow will cause us to be rejected by others. Shadow material tends to make us feel intensely uncomfortable, but to ignore our fear or anger or hurt is to negate a powerful source of wisdom. The insects with the highest "ick" factor are often our greatest Shadow teachers.

Shadow material tends to make us feel intensely uncomfortable, but to ignore our fear or anger or hurt is to negate a powerful source of wisdom. The insects with the highest "ick" factor are often our greatest Shadow teachers.

Bedbugs

Bedbugs have gained much notoriety in recent years, though the bedtime blessing "Don't let the bedbugs bite" has been a familiar refrain since the 1880s, and these tiny vampiric bugs have made nighttime a nightmare for thousands of years. As teachers, they invite us to look at negative patterns in our lives, especially disruptive rhythms that keep us from reaching our full potential.

Centipedes and Millipedes

I have a theory that, as humans, we are great with anything that has two legs, fine with four legs, on the fence about six legs, highly uncertain about eight legs, and decidedly repulsed by a hundred or a thousand legs. Centipedes and millipedes live in dark, musty places or crawl out of drains when we least expect it, and they move fast! As Shadow teachers, they alert us to the need for transformation, particularly if and when we are resistant to it. They can also guide us in being open to psychic development.

Cockroaches

One of the most well-known of the Shadow teachers, the cockroach is one of the insects we tend to dislike the most. Many people are familiar with the belief that only cockroaches could survive a nuclear war. They can live without food—and even without their heads!—for weeks. There is an association with filth and infestation that makes our skin crawl when pondering this hard-shelled teacher, but there is almost no better guide when it comes to teaching us how to survive in the face of extreme adversity and how to adapt ourselves to thrive in any circumstance.

Locusts and Grasshoppers

Having marched through history with tales of voracious, destructive plagues, locusts and grasshoppers have never been loved by farmers. The infamous Grasshopper Plague of 1874 covered Kansas so completely that it is said the sun was blocked from the sky. Crops, sheep's wool, and even clothes off people's backs were consumed, leaving the Kansan settlers in a state of destitution. Despite these devastating plagues, the grasshopper teaches us how to seize opportunities wherever they present themselves, always moving forward and leaving what is barren behind us.

Termites

Unlike the benign nuisance of ants, the presence of termites in a house can spell disaster. Termites will consume all cellulose-based plant material and not just wood, which opens up worlds of furniture, foundations, filtration systems, and more to their powerful jaws. Intensely social, they teach us the power of working in groups and honing dedication to bring a task to completion.

Industrious Insects We Admire

All insects are, in truth, incredibly hard-working, but there are certain ones that we tend to view with neutral respect. They don't necessarily repulse us, but we also don't tend to embrace them as beloved teachers.

Ants

Though we may not love to see an army of ants in our homes, these insects aren't particularly destructive. Ants are renowned for their incredible strength. The leafcutter ant can carry an object in its jaws that is fifty times its body weight. Not only are ants teachers in matters of focus and community, but they also encourage us to tap previously unknown stores of fortitude.

Cicadas

The buzzing hum that fills the air on hot summer days without an obvious source is the sound of male cicadas calling to the females. Their song sings to us of respecting our own natural rhythms and being open to hearing hidden truths.

Wasps

Wasps have a reputation for having a nasty temper, particularly the yellow jackets, and as such they can teach us about standing up for ourselves. But they are also master builders and have much to teach us about effective construction and productivity.

Inspiring Insects We Love

Many insects beguile us with their beauty. Glowing with captivating colors or awe-inspiring designs, these insects bring to mind the magic of the faery world. For many, these are the Light teachers, and we tend to be happy to work with them.

Bees

As master communicators, bees reflect the importance of conveying accurate information. They teach us to seek new avenues of knowledge, especially those that open us to experiencing the sweetness of life. In particular, the physics-defying bumblebee shows us how to be our wonderful, impossible selves, regardless of what others may think.

Butterflies

Probably the most universally loved insect, the butterfly is best known as a symbol of transformation, in reference to the change from caterpillar to butterfly that occurs within the safety of the cocoon. Many people also feel that butterflies indicate the presence of deceased loved

ones and spirit guides. The monarch butterfly encourages endurance, reflective of its migration from Canada and the northern United States to central Mexico, an incredible trip made twice a year.

Crickets

Crickets have long been loved in China as bringers of good fortune. An especially loud cricket indicates prosperity. For almost a thousand years, they were also loved for their "song" to such an extent that crickets were housed in specially designed cages to be kept as pets. Also nocturnal omnivores, katydids present a similar message.

Dragonflies and Damselflies

Dragonflies and damselflies are often confused with each other. Dragonflies have broad bodies with forewings and hindwings that are different shapes. Damselflies have narrow bodies, looking almost like an iridescent stick with wings. Both, however, are totems that help us break through illusion, to see the truth and open us to swift change.

Fireflies

There is almost nothing as magical as a summer firefly light show. With its playful meadow dance, the firefly awakens the child within, sparking joy and curiosity in order for us to pursue our passion. As the most highly efficient light producers, they teach us how to work with focus and efficacy.

Moths

Though the often drab moth tends to play second fiddle to the colorful butterfly, its nocturnal nature guides us to seek the light in the dark. Rather than transforming dark into light, the moth helps us find the gifts in whatever challenges or scares us.

Insects with a Story

Considering that insects predate humans by millions of years and are an inextricable part of the human experience, it is to be expected that many of them crop up in myths and folklore across the world.

Mantises

Mantises, related to termites and cockroaches, were considered to have supernatural powers by ancient peoples. An early Chinese reference praised the mantis's courage and fearlessness. Perhaps the best known mantis is the praying mantis, which teaches us how to embrace stillness and open ourselves to divine intervention.

Dung Beetles

It's a little harder to see a divine connection with the maligned dung beetle, yet the scarab (or *kheper*, as it was called by the Egyptians) was the most popular protective amulet in ancient Egypt. Used extensively by pharaohs, the scarab symbolized the sun god Ra and the movement of the sun across the sky, resurrecting itself each and every day.

Ladybugs

Contrary to the rather depressing nursery rhyme that bears its name, the humble ladybird (or ladybug) carries the distinction in British folklore of having the ability to carry away illness and trouble. It bestows abundance and grants wishes.

Honorary Insects

Even though arachnids are not of the insect family, we have a tendency to view them as such. As "honorary" insects, these totems tend to be Shadow teachers, guiding us to reclaim empowerment from whatever we would prefer to avoid.

Mites

Tiny mites are said to be the most successful of the invertebrates. Incredibly diverse and ranging from small to microscopic, they thrive everywhere. Mites teach us to be respectful of people and things that are very small. Persistence has the ability to overthrow a giant.

Scorpions

The potent and sometimes terrifying scorpion has the distinction of being the only insect found in the zodiac (Scorpio). Best known in mythology as Orion's rival, Scorpio was created by Gaia to fulfill the task of bringing down the boastful Orion. Vigilance and defense are the lessons of the scorpion.

SPIDERS

The spider is another master architect, creating masterpieces with thread. Perseverance, creativity, and weaving have long been associated with spiders, but there is also the element of respecting interconnections and honoring communication. There is no part of a web that is not intricately connected to another. To twang one strand is to send a message throughout the whole complex. In many ways, bees and spiders work to similar ends.

. . . .

The next time one of these tiny teachers finds its way to you, resist the impulse to swat it away. As with any other totem, listen to its wisdom and hear its message for you at that moment in your life. This is not to say that every bug need stop you in its tracks. But as with other totems, if an insect makes a significant or unusual appearance in your day, it is very likely that Spirit has shown up in miniscule form to enlighten you.

Tiffany Lazic *is a* Registered Psychotherapist *and* Spiritual Director *with a private practice in individual, couples, and group therapy. As the owner of the* Hive and Grove Centre for Holistic Wellness, *she created two self-development programs focused on teaching inner alchemy and intuitive tools from around the world and is a staff facilitator in the* Transformational Arts College of Spiritual and Holistic Training's Spiritual Directorship and Esoteric Studies Programs. *She is an international presenter and retreat facilitator and the founder of* Kitchener's Red Tent Temple, *and she serves on the* Council of the Sisterhood of Avalon. *Tiffany is the author of* The Great Work: Self-Knowledge and Healing Through the Wheel of the Year. *Visit her at www.hiveandgrove.ca.*

Illustrator: Jennifer Hewitson

Courting the Dark Side: Finding a Balance Between Light and Shadow

Laurel Reufner

I have a secret to let you all in on: I'm a reformed people-pleaser as well as a sufferer of an over-active guilty conscious. I'm not saying that guilt is a bad thing—not in its proper place. It can certainly help keep us in line when it comes to how we treat others. But it's also possible to let guilt hold us back from more fully enjoying life and being who we are. And that's a problem that lies within our shadow self—our dark side—first identified by Sigmund Freud and Carl Jung.

Freud described the unconscious as a place where we store all of our repressed

ideas and emotions. However, those ideas and emotions don't always stay put. Sometimes they resurface into our conscious mind, usually when we least need them to. Jung took this concept several steps further by describing the shadow as a spot where we place (repress) all of our dark thoughts and desires—things we think of as sinful. Entire books and many academic papers have been written on Jungian psychology and the nature of the shadow, but this definition will serve well enough for our purposes here.

Many of us come to Paganism from different spiritual or religious paths, ones that are usually a bit more dualistic (good vs. evil) in their theology. This isn't necessarily an attack on those paths. I mean, we all want to be considered good, right? So what do you do when you don't feel that a particular impulse or emotion is considered good? If we could just shove those bad things down in our minds deeply enough, we could bury them and forget all about them. We could win out over this dark side. Except that's not really how it works. In order to reach wholeness and ultimately be a better person, we need to embrace our shadow and learn to work with it.

Denying our shadow, at the very least, keeps us from enjoying the full emotional range of life and at its worst leads to violence, addiction, and alienation. We become adversarial within ourselves, but we don't have to do that.

My goal here is to give you some insight into making friends with your darker side. All too often, not only do we put dark, sinful thoughts into our shadow, but it's also where we sometimes put useful emotions and thoughts, all because we may find them uncomfortable. Fear of all sorts can find a home in our shadow, as well as pride and confidence in ourselves. Sometimes we might even hide love in there. What's a Witch to do? What Witches often do: try to deal with it head-on.

Making Friends with Your Shadow

Where do you start getting those impulses under control and begin embracing your shadow side? For me, it was a case of acknowledging certain feelings, especially when I would feel guilty about things that a person really shouldn't feel guilty about. You know, things that would be perfectly acceptable in other people. If I wouldn't think badly of someone else for saying that they couldn't do a certain thing or for rightly standing their ground, then why the heck should I feel guilty about it in myself? Of course, the reasons for my overly developed guilty conscience go way back to my youth, which is something that still needs work—but I'm getting there.

I've learned to pay attention to when I'm feeling guilty about something and seek out the reason for it. Then I keep repeating the following mantra for as long as I need to: *If it wouldn't bother me if it were someone else, then it probably shouldn't bother me.* This is a tactic that works well for other emotions as well. And sometimes, feeling a little guilty does get me to do something that I should be doing, such as getting off my duff and surprising my family with a special home-cooked meal. If I'm really tired, they'll understand if I don't, but if I'm just being lazy that's another matter. (A big part of this process is learning to be honest, at least with yourself.)

Something else that helps is working to untangle why you feel a certain way. And by that, I mean taking the emotion back to the source. Do you find it hard to take pride in yourself because you've long been told that pridefulness is wrong and you've taken that message a little too much to heart? While excessive pridefulness is a problem, taking pride in a job well done is a very healthy thing for your self-confidence.

You also need to pay attention to when your shadow is trying to protect you. Perhaps you're afraid of personal relationships because you're really afraid of being hurt or rejected. So instead you live your life lonely and cut off from forming close relationships, maybe even

becoming bitter and resentful of those around you who have what you're so afraid to try for. Maybe you were rejected once by someone for whom you cared deeply and you don't ever want to feel that way again, so your shadow tries to give you that protection by keeping you afraid and isolated. Tackle this problem by acknowledging the fear and realizing that your dark psyche is only trying to help you. Then take small steps to get out there and meet people.

Pay attention to that little voice when it starts to speak up, listen to what it's saying, and then ask yourself where that emotion is really coming from. What is your shadow trying to protect you from? What might it be trying to tell you? Why do you feel bad about feeling perfectly normal human emotions that we all have?

One final suggestion is to start a practice of mindfulness or perhaps meditation. In those moments of inner stillness, realizations and enlightenment might come to you. For me, it's the stillness of the night and maybe some contemplative candlelight or a good long drive over roads I know well that often lead to a mental calmness that lets me sort out my thoughts and feelings. Part of my mind can then wander about inside itself and discover thoughts that I had no idea existed.

Of course, these suggestions are only starting points, and sometimes we all need a little extra, professional help. If you decide that's the case, then please don't hesitate to go get some. There is no shame in acknowledging when you need assistance. Knowing when to do so can be a true sign of strength.

Laurel Reufner *loves writing about all sorts of topics. An observer of human nature, she found the topic of this particular article to be truly fascinating and enlightening. Many thanks go out to reader Claudette for suggesting it. When not lost in her own head, she lives in beautiful southeastern Ohio, with her husband and two rapidly growing teenage daughters, who both continue her wild child legacy. Visit her on Facebook.*

Illustrator: Rik Olson

The Lunar Calendar

September 2017 to December 2018

SEPTEMBER

S	M	T	W	T	F	S
					1	2
3	4	5	6	7	8	9
10	11	12	13	14	15	16
17	18	19	20	21	22	23
24	25	26	27	28	29	30

OCTOBER

S	M	T	W	T	F	S
1	2	3	4	5	6	7
8	9	10	11	12	13	14
15	16	17	18	19	20	21
22	23	24	25	26	27	28
29	30	31				

NOVEMBER

S	M	T	W	T	F	S
			1	2	3	4
5	6	7	8	9	10	11
12	13	14	15	16	17	18
19	20	21	22	23	24	25
26	27	28	29	30		

DECEMBER

S	M	T	W	T	F	S
					1	2
3	4	5	6	7	8	9
10	11	12	13	14	15	16
17	18	19	20	21	22	23
24	25	26	27	28	29	30
31						

2018

JANUARY

S	M	T	W	T	F	S
	1	2	3	4	5	6
7	8	9	10	11	12	13
14	15	16	17	18	19	20
21	22	23	24	25	26	27
28	29	30	31			

FEBRUARY

S	M	T	W	T	F	S
				1	2	3
4	5	6	7	8	9	10
11	12	13	14	15	16	17
18	19	20	21	22	23	24
25	26	27	28			

MARCH

S	M	T	W	T	F	S
				1	2	3
4	5	6	7	8	9	10
11	12	13	14	15	16	17
18	19	20	21	22	23	24
25	26	27	28	29	30	31

APRIL

S	M	T	W	T	F	S
1	2	3	4	5	6	7
8	9	10	11	12	13	14
15	16	17	18	19	20	21
22	23	24	25	26	27	28
29	30					

MAY

S	M	T	W	T	F	S
		1	2	3	4	5
6	7	8	9	10	11	12
13	14	15	16	17	18	19
20	21	22	23	24	25	26
27	28	29	30	31		

JUNE

S	M	T	W	T	F	S
					1	2
3	4	5	6	7	8	9
10	11	12	13	14	15	16
17	18	19	20	21	22	23
24	25	26	27	28	29	30

JULY

S	M	T	W	T	F	S
1	2	3	4	5	6	7
8	9	10	11	12	13	14
15	16	17	18	19	20	21
22	23	24	25	26	27	28
29	30	31				

AUGUST

S	M	T	W	T	F	S
			1	2	3	4
5	6	7	8	9	10	11
12	13	14	15	16	17	18
19	20	21	22	23	24	25
26	27	28	29	30	31	

SEPTEMBER

S	M	T	W	T	F	S
						1
2	3	4	5	6	7	8
9	10	11	12	13	14	15
16	17	18	19	20	21	22
23	24	25	26	27	28	29
30						

OCTOBER

S	M	T	W	T	F	S
	1	2	3	4	5	6
7	8	9	10	11	12	13
14	15	16	17	18	19	20
21	22	23	24	25	26	27
28	29	30	31			

NOVEMBER

S	M	T	W	T	F	S
				1	2	3
4	5	6	7	8	9	10
11	12	13	14	15	16	17
18	19	20	21	22	23	24
25	26	27	28	29	30	

DECEMBER

S	M	T	W	T	F	S
						1
2	3	4	5	6	7	8
9	10	11	12	13	14	15
16	17	18	19	20	21	22
23	24	25	26	27	28	29
30	31					

SEPTEMBER 2017

SU	M	T	W
27	28	29	30
3 2nd ♒	4 2nd ♒ *Labor Day*	5 2nd ♒ ☽ v/c 1:15 am ☽ → ♓ 1:28 am ☿ D 7:29 am *Mercury direct*	6 2nd ♓ Full Moon 3:03 am ☽ v/c 4:29 pm *Harvest Moon*
10 3rd ♉ ☽ v/c 8:54 pm	11 3rd ♉ ☽ → ♊ 3:29 pm	12 3rd ♊	13 3rd ♊ 4th Quarter 2:25 am ☽ v/c 2:35 pm ☽ → ♋ 6:12 pm
17 4th ♌ ☽ v/c 8:55 pm	18 4th ♌ ☽ → ♍ 12:52 am	19 4th ♍	20 4th ♍ ☽ v/c 1:30 am New Moon 1:30 am ☽ → ♎ 6:06 am *New Moon*
24 1st ♏ ☽ v/c 3:33 am	25 1st ♏ ☽ → ♐ 12:01 am	26 1st ♐	27 1st ♐ ☽ v/c 7:08 am ☽ → ♑ 12:24 pm 2nd Quarter 10:54 pm
1	2	3	4

Eastern Daylight Time (EDT)

Zodiac Signs

♈ Aries, ♉ Taurus, ♊ Gemini, ♋ Cancer, ♌ Leo, ♍ Virgo, ♎ Libra, ♏ Scorpio, ♐ Sagittarius, ♑ Capricorn, ♒ Aquarius, ♓ Pisces

Planets

☉ Sun, ☽ Moon, ☿ Mercury, ♀ Venus, ♂ Mars, ♃ Jupiter, ♄ Saturn, ♅ Uranus, ♆ Neptune, ♇ Pluto

SEPTEMBER 2017

TH	F	SA	NOTES
31	2nd ♑ 1	2nd ♑ 2 ☽ v/c 12:30 pm ☽ → ♒ 4:06 pm	
3rd ♓ 7 ☽ → ♈ 8:01 am	3rd ♈ 8	3rd ♈ 9 ☽ v/c 11:52 am ☽ → ♉ 12:23 pm	
4th ♋ 14	4th ♋ 15 ☽ v/c 5:23 pm ☽ → ♌ 9:09 pm	4th ♌ 16	
1st ♎ 21	1st ♎ 22 ☽ v/c 9:04 am ☽ → ♏ 1:40 pm ☉ → ♎ 4:02 pm *Mabon* *Sun enters Libra* *Fall Equinox*	1st ♏ 23	
2nd ♑ 28	2nd ♑ 29 ☽ v/c 8:14 pm	2nd ♑ 30 ☽ → ♒ 12:40 am	
5	6	7	

Aspects & Moon Phases

☌ Conjunction	0°	● New Moon	(1st Quarter)
⚹ Sextile	60°	◐ Waxing Moon	(2nd Quarter)
□ Square	90°	○ Full Moon	(3rd Quarter)
△ Trine	120°	◑ Waning Moon	(4th Quarter)
⚻ Quincunx	150°		
☍ Opposition	180°		

OCTOBER 2017

SU	M	T	W
1 2nd ♒	2 2nd ♒ ☽ v/c 7:13 am ☽ → ♓ 10:26 am	3 2nd ♓	4 2nd ♓ ☽ v/c 3:19 am ☽ → ♈ 4:40 pm
8 3rd ♉ ☽ v/c 9:45 am ☽ → ♊ 9:44 pm	9 3rd ♊	10 3rd ♊ ☽ v/c 6:25 pm ☽ → ♋ 11:38 pm	11 3rd ♋
15 4th ♌ ☽ v/c 1:28 am ☽ → ♍ 7:19 am	16 4th ♍	17 4th ♍ ☽ v/c 7:27 am ☽ → ♎ 1:35 pm	18 4th ♎
22 1st ♏ ☽ v/c 7:35 am ☽ → ♐ 7:57 am	23 1st ♐ ☉ → ♏ 1:27 am *Sun enters Scorpio*	24 1st ♐ ☽ v/c 12:44 pm ☽ → ♑ 8:12 pm	25 1st ♑
29 2nd ♒ ☽ v/c 12:22 pm ☽ → ♓ 7:46 pm	30 2nd ♓	31 2nd ♓ ☽ v/c 5:08 pm *Samhain* *Halloween*	1
5	6	7	8

Eastern Daylight Time (EDT)

Zodiac Signs

♈ Aries
♉ Taurus
♊ Gemini
♋ Cancer
♌ Leo
♍ Virgo
♎ Libra
♏ Scorpio
♐ Sagittarius
♑ Capricorn
♒ Aquarius
♓ Pisces

Planets

☉ Sun
☽ Moon
☿ Mercury
♀ Venus
♂ Mars
♃ Jupiter
♄ Saturn
♅ Uranus
♆ Neptune
♇ Pluto

OCTOBER 2017

TH	F	SA	NOTES
2nd ♈ ○ Full Moon 2:40 pm *Blood Moon*	6 3rd ♈ ☽ v/c 6:38 pm ☽ → ♉ 7:56 pm	7 3rd ♉	
3rd ♋ ◑ 4th Quarter 8:25 am	13 4th ♋ ☽ v/c 12:00 am ☽ → ♌ 2:41 am	14 4th ♌	
4th ♎ ● ☽ v/c 3:12 pm New Moon 3:12 pm ☽ → ♏ 9:41 pm *New Moon*	20 1st ♏	21 1st ♏	
26 1st ♑	1st ♑ ◐ ☽ v/c 1:22 am ☽ → ♒ 8:59 am 2nd Quarter 6:22 pm	28 2nd ♒	
2	3	4	
9	10	11	

Aspects & Moon Phases

☌ Conjunction	0°	● New Moon	(1st Quarter)
✶ Sextile	60°	◐ Waxing Moon	(2nd Quarter)
□ Square	90°	○ Full Moon	(3rd Quarter)
△ Trine	120°	◑ Waning Moon	(4th Quarter)
⚻ Quincunx	150°		
☍ Opposition	180°		

NOVEMBER 2017

SU	M	T	W
29	30	31	1 2nd ♓ ☽ → ♈ 2:43 am
5 3rd ♉ ☽ v/c 4:29 am ☽ → ♊ 5:26 am *Daylight Saving Time ends at 2:00 am*	6 3rd ♊	7 3rd ♊ ☽ v/c 5:40 am ☽ → ♋ 5:45 am *Election Day (general)*	8 3rd ♋
12 4th ♍	11 4th ♍ ☽ v/c 10:45 am ☽ → ♎ 6:26 pm	14 4th ♎	15 4th ♎ ☽ v/c 7:50 pm
19 1st ♐	20 1st ♐ ☽ v/c 7:26 pm	21 1st ♐ ☽ → ♑ 2:14 am ☉ → ♐ 10:05 pm *Sun enters Sagittarius*	22 1st ♑
◐ 1st ♒ ☽ → ♓ 3:04 am 2nd Quarter 12:03 pm	27 2nd ♓	28 2nd ♓ ☽ v/c 7:09 am ☽ → ♈ 11:30 am	29 2nd ♈
3	4	5	6

Eastern Daylight Time (EDT) becomes Eastern Standard Time (EST) November 5

Zodiac Signs

♈ Aries
♉ Taurus
♊ Gemini
♋ Cancer
♌ Leo
♍ Virgo
♎ Libra
♏ Scorpio
♐ Sagittarius
♑ Capricorn
♒ Aquarius
♓ Pisces

Planets

☉ Sun
☽ Moon
☿ Mercury
♀ Venus
♂ Mars
♃ Jupiter
♄ Saturn
♅ Uranus
♆ Neptune
♇ Pluto

NOVEMBER 2017

TH	F	SA	NOTES
2 — 2nd ♈ ☽ v/c 11:03 pm	3 — 2nd ♈ ☽ → ♉ 5:46 am	○ — 2nd ♉ Full Moon 1:23 am *Mourning Moon*	
9 — 3rd ♋ ☽ v/c 12:14 am ☽ → ♌ 7:29 am	◑ — 3rd ♌ 4th Quarter 3:36 pm	11 — 4th ♌ ☽ v/c 3:55 am ☽ → ♍ 11:41 am	
16 — 4th ♎ ☽ → ♏ 3:19 am	17 — 4th ♏	● — 4th ♏ ☽ v/c 6:42 am New Moon 6:42 am ☽ → ♐ 1:59 pm *New Moon*	
23 — 1st ♑ ☽ v/c 5:33 am ☽ → ♒ 3:14 pm *Thanksgiving Day*	24 — 1st ♒	25 — 1st ♒ ☽ v/c 9:37 pm	
30 — 2nd ♈ ☽ v/c 1:37 pm ☽ → ♉ 3:38 pm	1	2	
7	8	9	

Aspects & Moon Phases

☌ Conjunction	0°	● New Moon	(1st Quarter)
⚹ Sextile	60°	◐ Waxing Moon	(2nd Quarter)
□ Square	90°	○ Full Moon	(3rd Quarter)
△ Trine	120°	◑ Waning Moon	(4th Quarter)
⚻ Quincunx	150°		
☍ Opposition	180°		

DECEMBER 2017

SU	M	T	W
26	27	28	29
3 2nd ♊ ☿℞ 2:34 am Full Moon 10:47 am *Mercury retrograde* *Long Nights Moon*	4 3rd ♊ ☽ v/c 2:13 pm ☽ → ♋ 3:37 pm	5 3rd ♋	6 3rd ♋ ☽ v/c 12:56 pm ☽ → ♌ 3:37 pm
10 3rd ♍ 4th Quarter 2:51 am ☽ v/c 10:02 pm	11 4th ♍ ☽ → ♎ 12:01 am	12 4th ♎	13 4th ♎ ☽ v/c 7:27 am ☽ → ♏ 8:59 am
17 4th ♐	18 4th ♐ New Moon 1:30 am ☽ v/c 8:10 am ☽ → ♑ 8:33 am *New Moon*	19 1st ♑	20 1st ♑ ☽ v/c 10:37 am ☽ → ♒ 9:29 pm
24 1st ♓ ☽ v/c 9:48 pm *Christmas Eve*	25 1st ♓ ☽ → ♈ 7:27 pm *Christmas Day*	26 1st ♈ 2nd Quarter 4:20 am	27 2nd ♈ ☽ v/c 3:57 pm
31 2nd ♊ ☽ v/c 6:38 pm *New Year's Eve*	1	2	3

Eastern Standard Time (EST)

Zodiac Signs

♈ Aries
♉ Taurus
♊ Gemini
♋ Cancer
♌ Leo
♍ Virgo
♎ Libra
♏ Scorpio
♐ Sagittarius
♑ Capricorn
♒ Aquarius
♓ Pisces

Planets

☉ Sun
☽ Moon
☿ Mercury
♀ Venus
♂ Mars
♃ Jupiter
♄ Saturn
♅ Uranus
♆ Neptune
♇ Pluto

DECEMBER 2017

TH	F	SA	NOTES
30	1 2nd ♉ ☽ v/c 8:53 pm	2 2nd ♉ ☽ → ♊ 4:21 pm	
7 3rd ♌	8 3rd ♌ ☽ v/c 5:40 pm ☽ → ♍ 6:09 pm	9 3rd ♍	
14 4th ♏ ☽ v/c 8:42 pm	15 4th ♏ ☽ → ♐ 8:07 pm	16 4th ♐	
21 1st ♒ ☉ → ♑ 11:28 am *Yule* *Sun enters Capricorn* *Winter Solstice*	22 1st ♒ ☿ D 8:51 pm *Mercury direct*	23 1st ♒ ☽ v/c 5:13 am ☽ → ♓ 9:42 am	
28 2nd ♈ ☽ → ♉ 1:23 am	29 2nd ♉ ☽ v/c 9:01 am	30 2nd ♉ ☽ → ♊ 3:31 am	
4	5	6	

Aspects & Moon Phases

☌	Conjunction	0°
⚹	Sextile	60°
□	Square	90°
△	Trine	120°
⚻	Quincunx	150°
☍	Opposition	180°

●	New Moon	(1st Quarter)
◐	Waxing Moon	(2nd Quarter)
○	Full Moon	(3rd Quarter)
◑	Waning Moon	(4th Quarter)

JANUARY 2018

SU	M	T	W
31	2nd ♊ ☽ → ♋ 3:10 am Full Moon 9:24 pm ○ *New Year's Day* *Cold Moon*	3rd ♋ 2 ☽ v/c 5:46 pm	3rd ♋ 3 ☽ → ♌ 2:23 am
3rd ♍ 7 ☽ → ♎ 7:15 am	3rd ♎ ◑ 4th Quarter 5:25 pm	4th ♎ 9 ☽ v/c 11:13 am ☽ → ♏ 3:05 pm	4th ♏ 10
4th ♐ 14 ☽ v/c 3:48 am ☽ → ♑ 2:42 pm	4th ♑ 15 *Martin Luther King Jr. Day*	4th ♑ ● New Moon 9:17 pm *New Moon*	1st ♑ 17 ☽ v/c 1:30 am ☽ → ♒ 3:32 am
1st ♓ 21 ☽ v/c 8:13 pm	1st ♓ 22 ☽ → ♈ 1:27 am	1st ♈ 23 ☽ v/c 11:16 pm	1st ♈ ◐ ☽ → ♉ 8:39 am 2nd Quarter 5:20 pm
2nd ♊ 28 ☽ v/c 5:39 am ☽ → ♋ 1:57 pm	2nd ♋ 29	2nd ♋ 30 ☽ v/c 11:40 am ☽ → ♌ 1:53 pm	2nd ♌ ○ Full Moon 8:27 am *Blue Moon* *Lunar Eclipse*
4	5	6	7

Eastern Standard Time (EST)

Zodiac Signs

♈ Aries ♉ Taurus ♊ Gemini ♋ Cancer
♌ Leo ♍ Virgo ♎ Libra ♏ Scorpio
♐ Sagittarius ♑ Capricorn ♒ Aquarius ♓ Pisces

Planets

☉ Sun ☽ Moon ☿ Mercury ♀ Venus ♂ Mars
♃ Jupiter ♄ Saturn ♅ Uranus ♆ Neptune ♇ Pluto

JANUARY 2018

TH	F	SA	NOTES
4 3rd ♌ ☽ v/c 6:10 pm	5 3rd ♌ ☽ → ♍ 3:12 am	6 3rd ♍ ☽ v/c 9:51 pm	
11 4th ♏ ☽ v/c 9:53 am	12 4th ♏ ☽ → ♐ 2:04 am	13 4th ♐	
18 1st ♒	19 1st ♒ ☽ v/c 6:52 am ☽ → ♓ 3:26 pm ☉ → ♒ 10:09 pm *Sun enters Aquarius*	20 1st ♓	
25 2nd ♉ ☽ v/c 10:17 pm	26 2nd ♉ ☽ → ♊ 12:40 pm	27 2nd ♊	
1	2	3	
8	9	10	

Aspects & Moon Phases

☌ Conjunction	0°	● New Moon	(1st Quarter)
⚹ Sextile	60°	◐ Waxing Moon	(2nd Quarter)
□ Square	90°	○ Full Moon	(3rd Quarter)
△ Trine	120°	◑ Waning Moon	(4th Quarter)
⚻ Quincunx	150°		
☍ Opposition	180°		

FEBRUARY 2018

SU	M	T	W
28	29	30	31
4 3rd ♎	5 3rd ♎ ☽ v/c 1:46 pm ☽ → ♏ 10:56 pm	6 3rd ♏	7 3rd ♏ 4th Quarter 10:54 am ◑
11 4th ♑	12 4th ♑	13 4th ♑ ☽ v/c 12:43 am ☽ → ♒ 10:11 am	14 4th ♒ *Valentine's Day*
18 1st ♓ ☽ → ♈ 7:05 am ☉ → ♓ 12:18 pm *Sun enters Pisces*	19 1st ♈ *Presidents' Day*	20 1st ♈ ☽ v/c 6:11 am ☽ → ♉ 2:12 pm	21 1st ♉
25 2nd ♋	26 2nd ♋ ☽ v/c 4:51 pm ☽ → ♌ 11:42 pm	27 2nd ♌	28 2nd ♌ ☽ v/c 6:13 pm
4	5	6	7

Eastern Standard Time (EST)

Zodiac Signs

♈ Aries
♉ Taurus
♊ Gemini
♋ Cancer
♌ Leo
♍ Virgo
♎ Libra
♏ Scorpio
♐ Sagittarius
♑ Capricorn
♒ Aquarius
♓ Pisces

Planets

☉ Sun
☽ Moon
☿ Mercury
♀ Venus
♂ Mars
♃ Jupiter
♄ Saturn
♅ Uranus
♆ Neptune
♇ Pluto

FEBRUARY 2018

TH	F	SA	NOTES
1 3rd ♌ ☽ v/c 5:59 am ☽ → ♍ 2:13 pm	2 3rd ♍ *Imbolc* *Groundhog Day*	3 3rd ♍ ☽ v/c 2:07 am ☽ → ♎ 4:47 pm	
8 4th ♏ ☽ v/c 2:16 am ☽ → ♐ 8:53 am	9 4th ♐	10 4th ♐ ☽ v/c 11:38 am ☽ → ♑ 9:21 pm	
● 4th ♒ ☽ v/c 4:05 pm New Moon 4:05 pm ☽ → ♓ 9:42 pm *New Moon* *Solar Eclipse*	16 1st ♓	17 1st ♓ ☽ v/c 5:14 pm	
22 1st ♉ ☽ v/c 6:46 am ☽ → ♊ 7:07 pm	◐ 1st ♊ 2nd Quarter 3:09 am	24 2nd ♊ ☽ v/c 2:58 pm ☽ → ♋ 10:06 pm	
1	2	3	
8	9	10	

Aspects & Moon Phases

☌ Conjunction	0°	● New Moon	(1st Quarter)
⚹ Sextile	60°	◐ Waxing Moon	(2nd Quarter)
□ Square	90°	○ Full Moon	(3rd Quarter)
△ Trine	120°	◑ Waning Moon	(4th Quarter)
⚻ Quincunx	150°		
☍ Opposition	180°		

MARCH 2018

SU	M	T	W
25	26	27	28
4 3rd ♎	5 3rd ♎ ☽ v/c 1:19 am ☽ → ♏ 8:23 am	6 3rd ♏	7 3rd ♏ ☽ v/c 3:55 am ☽ → ♐ 5:03 pm
11 4th ♑ *Daylight Saving Time begins at 2:00 am*	12 4th ♑ ☽ v/c 11:36 am ☽ → ♒ 6:44 pm	13 4th ♒	14 4th ♒
18 1st ♈	19 1st ♈ ☽ v/c 3:29 pm ☽ → ♉ 9:07 pm	20 1st ♉ ☉ → ♈ 12:15 pm *Ostara* *Sun enters Aries* *Spring Equinox*	21 1st ♉ ☽ v/c 1:21 pm
25 2nd ♋	26 2nd ♋ ☽ v/c 2:58 am ☽ → ♌ 7:45 am	27 2nd ♌	28 2nd ♌ ☽ v/c 5:54 am ☽ → ♍ 10:30 am
1	2	3	4

Eastern Standard Time (EST) becomes Eastern Daylight Time (EDT) March 11

Zodiac Signs

♈ Aries ♉ Taurus ♊ Gemini ♋ Cancer
♌ Leo ♍ Virgo ♎ Libra ♏ Scorpio
♐ Sagittarius ♑ Capricorn ♒ Aquarius ♓ Pisces

Planets

☉ Sun ☽ Moon ☿ Mercury ♀ Venus ♂ Mars
♃ Jupiter ♄ Saturn ♅ Uranus ♆ Neptune ♇ Pluto

MARCH 2018

TH	F	SA	NOTES
○ 2nd ♌ ☽ → ♍ 12:57 am Full Moon 7:51 pm *Storm Moon*	2 3rd ♍ ☽ v/c 6:50 pm	3 3rd ♍ ☽ → ♎ 3:20 am	
8 3rd ♐	◑ 3rd ♐ 4th Quarter 6:20 am ☽ v/c 9:27 pm	10 4th ♐ ☽ → ♑ 4:52 am	
15 4th ♒ ☽ v/c 3:32 am ☽ → ♓ 6:12 am	16 4th ♓	● 4th ♓ ☽ v/c 9:12 am New Moon 9:12 am ☽ → ♈ 2:57 pm *St. Patrick's Day* *New Moon*	
22 1st ♉ ☽ → ♊ 1:30 am ☿℞ 8:19 pm *Mercury retrograde*	23 1st ♊ ☽ v/c 11:52 pm	◐ 1st ♊ ☽ → ♋ 4:53 am 2nd Quarter 11:35 am	
29 2nd ♍	30 2nd ♍ ☽ v/c 12:59 am ☽ → ♎ 1:52 pm	○ 2nd ♎ Full Moon 8:37 am *Blue Moon*	
5	6	7	

Aspects & Moon Phases

☌ Conjunction	0°	● New Moon	(1st Quarter)
⚹ Sextile	60°	◐ Waxing Moon	(2nd Quarter)
□ Square	90°	○ Full Moon	(3rd Quarter)
△ Trine	120°	◑ Waning Moon	(4th Quarter)
⚻ Quincunx	150°		
☍ Opposition	180°		

APRIL 2018

SU	M	T	W
3rd ♎ 1 ☽ v/c 2:29 pm ☽ → ♏ 6:57 pm *All Fools' Day*	3rd ♏ 2	3rd ♏ 3 ☽ v/c 12:06 pm	3rd ♏ 4 ☽ → ♐ 2:55 am
3rd ♑ 4th Quarter 3:18 am ☽ v/c 10:40 pm	4th ♑ 9 ☽ → ♒ 2:50 am	4th ♒ 10	4th ♒ 11 ☽ v/c 10:55 am ☽ → ♓ 2:40 pm
4th ♈ ☿ D 5:21 am New Moon 9:57 pm *Mercury direct* *New Moon*	1st ♈ 16 ☽ v/c 1:59 am ☽ → ♉ 4:51 am	1st ♉ 17 ☽ v/c 6:05 pm	1st ♉ 18 ☽ → ♊ 8:02 am
1st ♋ ☽ v/c 10:58 am ☽ → ♌ 1:09 pm 2nd Quarter 5:46 pm *Earth Day*	2nd ♌ 23	2nd ♌ 24 ☽ v/c 2:40 pm ☽ → ♍ 4:40 pm	2nd ♍ 25
2nd ♎ ☽ v/c 1:32 am ☽ → ♏ 3:11 am Full Moon 8:58 pm *Wind Moon*	3rd ♏ 30 ☽ v/c 10:56 pm	1	2
6	7	8	9

Eastern Daylight Time (EDT)

Zodiac Signs

♈ Aries, ♉ Taurus, ♊ Gemini, ♋ Cancer, ♌ Leo, ♍ Virgo, ♎ Libra, ♏ Scorpio, ♐ Sagittarius, ♑ Capricorn, ♒ Aquarius, ♓ Pisces

Planets

☉ Sun, ☽ Moon, ☿ Mercury, ♀ Venus, ♂ Mars, ♃ Jupiter, ♄ Saturn, ♅ Uranus, ♆ Neptune, ♇ Pluto

APRIL 2018

TH	F	SA	NOTES
3rd ♐ **5**	3rd ♐ **6** ☽ v/c 9:36 am ☽ → ♑ 2:01 pm	3rd ♑ **7**	
4th ♓ **12**	4th ♓ **13** ☽ v/c 7:27 am ☽ → ♈ 11:25 pm	4th ♈ **14**	
1st ♊ **19** ☉ → ♉ 11:13 pm *Sun enters Taurus*	1st ♊ **20** ☽ v/c 8:05 am ☽ → ♋ 10:26 am	1st ♋ **21**	
2nd ♍ **26** ☽ v/c 5:49 am ☽ → ♎ 9:13 pm	2nd ♎ **27**	2nd ♎ **28**	
3	4	5	
10	11	12	

Aspects & Moon Phases

☌ Conjunction	0°	● New Moon	(1st Quarter)
⚹ Sextile	60°	◐ Waxing Moon	(2nd Quarter)
□ Square	90°	○ Full Moon	(3rd Quarter)
△ Trine	120°	◑ Waning Moon	(4th Quarter)
⚻ Quincunx	150°		
☍ Opposition	180°		

MAY 2018

SU	M	T	W
29	30	1 3rd ♏ ☽ → ♐ 11:20 am *Beltane*	2 3rd ♐
6 3rd ♑ ☽ v/c 9:48 am ☽ → ♒ 10:48 am	7 3rd ♒ 4th Quarter 10:09 pm	8 4th ♒ ☽ v/c 10:29 pm ☽ → ♓ 11:11 pm	9 4th ♓
13 4th ♈ ☽ v/c 2:05 pm ☽ → ♉ 2:15 pm *Mother's Day*	14 4th ♉	15 4th ♉ New Moon 7:48 am ☽ v/c 4:30 pm ☽ → ♊ 4:43 pm *New Moon*	16 1st ♊
20 1st ♌ ☉ → ♊ 10:15 pm ☽ v/c 11:30 pm *Sun enters Gemini*	21 1st ♌ ☽ → ♍ 10:03 pm 2nd Quarter 11:49 pm	22 2nd ♍	23 2nd ♍ ☽ v/c 10:55 am
27 2nd ♏	28 2nd ♏ ☽ v/c 1:25 pm ☽ → ♐ 6:29 pm *Memorial Day*	29 2nd ♐ Full Moon 10:20 am *Flower Moon*	30 3rd ♐ ☽ v/c 2:26 am
3	4	5	6

Eastern Daylight Time (EDT)

Zodiac Signs

♈ Aries ♉ Taurus ♊ Gemini ♋ Cancer
♌ Leo ♍ Virgo ♎ Libra ♏ Scorpio
♐ Sagittarius ♑ Capricorn ♒ Aquarius ♓ Pisces

Planets

☉ Sun ☽ Moon ☿ Mercury ♀ Venus ♂ Mars
♃ Jupiter ♄ Saturn ♅ Uranus ♆ Neptune ♇ Pluto

MAY 2018

TH	F	SA	NOTES
3 3rd ♐ ☽ v/c 8:50 pm ☽ → ♑ 10:06 pm	4 3rd ♑	5 3rd ♑	
10 4th ♓	11 4th ♓ ☽ v/c 5:02 am ☽ → ♈ 8:40 am	12 4th ♈	
17 1st ♊ ☽ v/c 2:18 pm ☽ → ♋ 5:47 pm	18 1st ♋	19 1st ♋ ☽ v/c 5:14 pm ☽ → ♌ 7:11 pm	
24 2nd ♍ ☽ → ♎ 2:52 am	25 2nd ♎ ☽ v/c 5:04 pm	26 2nd ♎ ☽ → ♏ 9:39 am	
31 3rd ♐ ☽ → ♑ 5:27 am	1	2	
7	8	9	

Aspects & Moon Phases

☌ Conjunction	0°	● New Moon	(1st Quarter)
⚹ Sextile	60°	◐ Waxing Moon	(2nd Quarter)
□ Square	90°	○ Full Moon	(3rd Quarter)
△ Trine	120°	◑ Waning Moon	(4th Quarter)
⚻ Quincunx	150°		
☍ Opposition	180°		

JUNE 2018

SU	M	T	W
27	28	29	30
3 3rd ♒	4 3rd ♒ ☽ v/c 1:10 am	5 3rd ♒ ☽ → ♓ 6:53 am	◑ 3rd ♓ 4th Quarter 2:32 pm
10 4th ♈ ☽ → ♉ 12:04 am	11 4th ♉ ☽ v/c 11:29 pm	12 4th ♉ ☽ → ♊ 2:53 am	● 4th ♊ ☽ v/c 3:43 pm New Moon 3:43 pm *New Moon*
17 1st ♌ ☽ v/c 11:26 pm *Father's Day*	18 1st ♌ ☽ → ♍ 4:41 am	19 1st ♍	◐ 1st ♍ ☽ v/c 6:51 am 2nd Quarter 6:51 am ☽ → ♎ 8:29 am
24 2nd ♏ ☽ v/c 10:00 am	25 2nd ♏ ☽ → ♐ 12:29 am	26 2nd ♐ ☽ v/c 8:53 am ♂ ℞ 5:04 pm *Mars retrograde*	27 2nd ♐ ☽ → ♑ 11:52 am
1	2	3	4

Eastern Daylight Time (EDT)

Zodiac Signs

♈ Aries
♉ Taurus
♊ Gemini
♋ Cancer
♌ Leo
♍ Virgo
♎ Libra
♏ Scorpio
♐ Sagittarius
♑ Capricorn
♒ Aquarius
♓ Pisces

Planets

☉ Sun
☽ Moon
☿ Mercury
♀ Venus
♂ Mars
♃ Jupiter
♄ Saturn
♅ Uranus
♆ Neptune
♇ Pluto

JUNE 2018

TH	F	SA	NOTES
31	1 3rd ♑ ☽ v/c 11:37 pm	2 3rd ♑ ☽ → ♒ 6:06 pm	
7 4th ♓ ☽ v/c 2:35 am ☽ → ♈ 5:26 pm	8 4th ♈	9 4th ♈ ☽ v/c 3:37 pm	
14 1st ♊ ☽ → ♋ 3:20 am *Flag Day*	15 1st ♋ ☽ v/c 12:18 pm	16 1st ♋ ☽ → ♌ 3:21 am	
21 2nd ♎ ☉ → ♋ 6:07 am ☽ v/c 9:34 pm *Litha* *Sun enters Cancer* *Summer Solstice*	22 2nd ♎ ☽ → ♏ 3:11 pm	23 2nd ♏	
○ 2nd ♑ Full Moon 12:53 am *Strong Sun Moon*	29 3rd ♑ ☽ v/c 4:58 am	30 3rd ♑ ☽ → ♒ 12:37 am	
5	6	7	

Aspects & Moon Phases

☌	Conjunction	0°
⚹	Sextile	60°
□	Square	90°
△	Trine	120°
⚻	Quincunx	150°
☍	Opposition	180°

●	New Moon	(1st Quarter)
◐	Waxing Moon	(2nd Quarter)
○	Full Moon	(3rd Quarter)
◑	Waning Moon	(4th Quarter)

JULY 2018

SU	M	T	W
1 3rd ≈ ☽ v/c 6:56 pm	2 3rd ≈ ☽ → ♓ 1:31 pm	3 3rd ♓	4 3rd ♓ ☽ v/c 5:47 am *Independence Day*
8 4th ♉	9 4th ♉ ☽ v/c 12:09 pm ☽ → ♊ 12:58 pm	10 4th ♊ ☽ v/c 4:00 pm	11 4th ♊ ☽ → ♋ 1:59 pm
15 1st ♌ ☽ → ♍ 1:31 pm	16 1st ♍	17 1st ♍ ☽ v/c 6:50 am ☽ → ♎ 3:42 pm	18 1st ♎
22 2nd ♏ ☽ v/c 5:18 am ☽ → ♐ 6:12 am ☉ → ♌ 5:00 pm *Sun enters Leo*	23 2nd ♐	24 2nd ♐ ☽ v/c 4:22 am ☽ → ♑ 5:49 pm	25 2nd ♑
29 3rd ≈ ☽ v/c 5:25 am ☽ → ♓ 7:28 pm	30 3rd ♓	31 3rd ♓ ☽ v/c 6:42 pm	1
5	6	7	8

Eastern Daylight Time (EDT)

Zodiac Signs

♈ Aries
♉ Taurus
♊ Gemini
♋ Cancer
♌ Leo
♍ Virgo
♎ Libra
♏ Scorpio
♐ Sagittarius
♑ Capricorn
≈ Aquarius
♓ Pisces

Planets

☉ Sun
☽ Moon
☿ Mercury
♀ Venus
♂ Mars
♃ Jupiter
♄ Saturn
♅ Uranus
♆ Neptune
♇ Pluto

JULY 2018

TH	F	SA	NOTES
5 3rd ♓ ☽ → ♈ 12:50 am	6 ◑ 3rd ♈ 4th Quarter 3:51 am	7 4th ♈ ☽ v/c 3:09 am ☽ → ♉ 8:51 am	
12 ● 4th ♋ ☽ v/c 10:48 pm New Moon 10:48 pm *New Moon* *Solar Eclipse*	13 1st ♋ ☽ → ♌ 1:31 pm	14 1st ♌ ☽ v/c 7:12 pm	
19 ◐ 1st ♎ ☽ v/c 3:52 pm 2nd Quarter 3:52 pm ☽ → ♏ 9:13 pm	20 2nd ♏	21 2nd ♏	
26 2nd ♑ ☿ ℞ 1:02 am ☽ v/c 9:41 am *Mercury retrograde*	27 ○ 2nd ♑ ☽ → ♒ 6:41 am Full Moon 4:20 pm *Blessing Moon* *Lunar Eclipse*	28 3rd ♒	
2	3	4	
9	10	11	

Aspects & Moon Phases

☌	Conjunction	0°	●	New Moon	(1st Quarter)
⚹	Sextile	60°	◐	Waxing Moon	(2nd Quarter)
□	Square	90°	○	Full Moon	(3rd Quarter)
△	Trine	120°	◑	Waning Moon	(4th Quarter)
⚻	Quincunx	150°			
☍	Opposition	180°			

AUGUST 2018

SU	M	T	W
29	30	31	1 3rd ♓ ☽ → ♈ 6:54 am *Lammas*
5 4th ♉ ☽ v/c 7:46 pm ☽ → ♊ 9:32 pm	6 4th ♊	7 4th ♊ ☽ v/c 3:54 am	8 4th ♊ ☽ → ♋ 12:01 am
12 1st ♍	13 1st ♍	14 1st ♍ ☽ v/c 12:37 am ☽ → ♎ 12:57 am	15 1st ♎
19 2nd ♐ ☿ D 12:25 am *Mercury direct*	20 2nd ♐ ☽ v/c 7:47 pm	21 2nd ♐ ☽ → ♑ 12:00 am	22 2nd ♑
○ 2nd ♒ ☽ → ♓ 1:32 am Full Moon 7:56 am *Corn Moon*	27 3rd ♓ ♂ D 10:05 am *Mars direct*	28 3rd ♓ ☽ v/c 9:54 am ☽ → ♈ 12:35 pm	29 3rd ♈
2	3	4	5

Eastern Daylight Time (EDT)

Zodiac Signs

♈ Aries ♉ Taurus ♊ Gemini ♋ Cancer
♌ Leo ♍ Virgo ♎ Libra ♏ Scorpio
♐ Sagittarius ♑ Capricorn ♒ Aquarius ♓ Pisces

Planets

☉ Sun ☽ Moon ☿ Mercury ♀ Venus ♂ Mars
♃ Jupiter ♄ Saturn ♅ Uranus ♆ Neptune ♇ Pluto

AUGUST 2018

TH	F	SA	NOTES
2 3rd ♈ ☽ v/c 10:52 pm	**3** 3rd ♈ ☽ → ♉ 3:51 pm	**3** ◑ 3rd ♉ 4th Quarter 2:18 pm	
9 4th ♋ ☽ v/c 7:21 am	**10** 4th ♋ ☽ → ♌ 12:18 am	**11** ● 4th ♌ ☽ v/c 5:58 am New Moon 5:58 am ☽ → ♍ 11:59 pm *New Moon* *Solar Eclipse*	
16 1st ♎ ☽ v/c 3:56 am ☽ → ♏ 4:54 am	**17** 1st ♏	**18** ◐ 1st ♏ 2nd Quarter 3:49 am ☽ v/c 11:07 am ☽ → ♐ 12:45 pm	
23 2nd ♑ ☉ → ♍ 12:09 am ☽ v/c 10:19 am ☽ → ♒ 12:56 pm *Sun enters Virgo*	**24** 2nd ♒	**25** 2nd ♒ ☽ v/c 12:39 am	
30 3rd ♈ ☽ v/c 7:04 pm ☽ → ♉ 9:30 pm	**31** 3rd ♉	1	
6	7	8	

Aspects & Moon Phases

☌ Conjunction	0°	● New Moon	(1st Quarter)
⚹ Sextile	60°	◐ Waxing Moon	(2nd Quarter)
□ Square	90°	○ Full Moon	(3rd Quarter)
△ Trine	120°	◑ Waning Moon	(4th Quarter)
⚻ Quincunx	150°		
☍ Opposition	180°		

SEPTEMBER 2018

SU	M	T	W
26	27	28	29
3rd ♉ ☽ v/c 1:56 am ☽ → ♊ 4:02 am 4th Quarter 10:37 pm	3 4th ♊ *Labor Day*	4 4th ♊ ☽ v/c 2:37 am ☽ → ♋ 8:03 am	5 4th ♋
4th ♍ New Moon 2:01 pm *New Moon*	10 1st ♍ ☽ v/c 11:12 am ☽ → ♎ 11:20 am	11 1st ♎ ☽ v/c 6:58 pm	12 1st ♎ ☽ → ♏ 2:15 pm
1st ♐ ☽ v/c 7:15 pm 2nd Quarter 7:15 pm	17 2nd ♐ ☽ → ♑ 7:07 am	18 2nd ♑	19 2nd ♑ ☽ v/c 1:10 pm ☽ → ♒ 7:52 pm
23 2nd ♓	2nd ♓ ☽ v/c 1:26 am ☽ → ♈ 7:04 pm Full Moon 10:52 pm *Harvest Moon*	25 3rd ♈	26 3rd ♈ ☽ v/c 6:28 am
30 3rd ♊ ☽ v/c 11:38 am	1	2	3

Eastern Daylight Time (EDT)

Zodiac Signs

♈ Aries
♉ Taurus
♊ Gemini
♋ Cancer
♌ Leo
♍ Virgo
♎ Libra
♏ Scorpio
♐ Sagittarius
♑ Capricorn
♒ Aquarius
♓ Pisces

Planets

☉ Sun
☽ Moon
☿ Mercury
♀ Venus
♂ Mars
♃ Jupiter
♄ Saturn
♅ Uranus
♆ Neptune
♇ Pluto

SEPTEMBER 2018

TH	F	SA	NOTES
30	31	1 3rd ♉	
6 4th ♋ ☽ v/c 8:43 am ☽ → ♌ 9:54 am	7 4th ♌	8 4th ♌ ☽ v/c 9:31 am ☽ → ♍ 10:29 am	
13 1st ♏	14 1st ♏ ☽ v/c 4:54 am ☽ → ♐ 8:45 pm	15 1st ♐	
20 2nd ♒	21 2nd ♒ ☽ v/c 1:13 pm	22 2nd ♒ ☽ → ♓ 8:27 am ☉ → ♎ 9:54 pm *Mabon* *Sun enters Libra* *Fall Equinox*	
27 3rd ♈ ☽ → ♉ 3:16 am	28 3rd ♉ ☽ v/c 6:36 pm	29 3rd ♉ ☽ → ♊ 9:26 am	
4	5	6	

Aspects & Moon Phases

☌ Conjunction	0°	● New Moon	(1st Quarter)
⚹ Sextile	60°	◐ Waxing Moon	(2nd Quarter)
□ Square	90°	○ Full Moon	(3rd Quarter)
△ Trine	120°	◑ Waning Moon	(4th Quarter)
⚻ Quincunx	150°		
☍ Opposition	180°		

OCTOBER 2018

SU	M	T	W
30	1 3rd ♊ ☽ → ♋ 2:00 pm	2 3rd ♋ 4th Quarter 5:45 am ◑	3 4th ♋ ☽ v/c 4:33 am ☽ → ♌ 5:12 pm
7 4th ♍ ☽ v/c 10:03 am ☽ → ♎ 9:10 pm	8 4th ♎ New Moon 11:47 pm ● *New Moon*	9 1st ♎ ☽ v/c 4:50 am	10 1st ♎ ☽ → ♏ 12:09 am
14 1st ♐ ☽ → ♑ 3:17 pm	15 1st ♑	16 1st ♑ 2nd Quarter 2:02 pm ◐ ☽ v/c 5:49 pm	17 2nd ♑ ☽ → ♒ 3:36 am
21 2nd ♓ ☽ v/c 7:47 pm	22 2nd ♓ ☽ → ♈ 2:58 am	23 2nd ♈ ☉ → ♏ 7:22 am ☽ v/c 2:18 pm *Sun enters Scorpio*	24 2nd ♈ ☽ → ♉ 10:33 am Full Moon 12:45 pm ○ *Blood Moon*
28 3rd ♊ ☽ v/c 12:37 am ☽ → ♋ 7:27 pm	29 3rd ♋	30 3rd ♋ ☽ v/c 10:31 pm ☽ → ♌ 10:42 pm	31 3rd ♌ 4th Quarter 12:40 pm ◑ *Samhain* *Halloween*
4	5	6	7

Eastern Daylight Time (EDT)

Zodiac Signs

♈ Aries
♉ Taurus
♊ Gemini
♋ Cancer
♌ Leo
♍ Virgo
♎ Libra
♏ Scorpio
♐ Sagittarius
♑ Capricorn
♒ Aquarius
♓ Pisces

Planets

☉ Sun
☽ Moon
☿ Mercury
♀ Venus
♂ Mars
♃ Jupiter
♄ Saturn
♅ Uranus
♆ Neptune
♇ Pluto

OCTOBER 2018

TH	F	SA	NOTES
4th ♌ **4**	4th ♌ **5** ☽ v/c 7:34 am ♀ ℞ 3:04 pm ☽ → ♍ 7:19 pm *Venus retrograde*	4th ♍ **6**	
1st ♏ **11** ☽ v/c 7:12 pm	1st ♏ **12** ☽ → ♐ 5:53 am	1st ♐ **13** ☽ v/c 8:58 pm	
2nd ♒ **18**	2nd ♒ **19** ☽ v/c 8:27 am ☽ → ♓ 4:20 pm	2nd ♓ **20**	
3rd ♉ **25**	3rd ♉ **26** ☽ v/c 10:49 am ☽ → ♊ 3:41 pm	3rd ♊ **27**	
1	2	3	
8	9	10	

Aspects & Moon Phases

☌ Conjunction	0°	● New Moon	(1st Quarter)
⚹ Sextile	60°	◐ Waxing Moon	(2nd Quarter)
□ Square	90°	○ Full Moon	(3rd Quarter)
△ Trine	120°	◑ Waning Moon	(4th Quarter)
⚻ Quincunx	150°		
☍ Opposition	180°		

NOVEMBER 2018

SU	M	T	W
28	29	30	31
4 4th ♍ ☽ v/c 2:26 am ☽ → ♎ 4:01 am *Daylight Saving Time ends at 2:00 am*	5 4th ♎	6 4th ♎ ☽ v/c 3:19 am ☽ → ♏ 8:02 am *Election Day (general)*	● 4th ♏ New Moon 11:02 am *New Moon*
11 1st ♑	12 1st ♑	13 1st ♑ ☽ v/c 10:13 am ☽ → ♒ 10:45 am	14 1st ♒
18 2nd ♓ ☽ v/c 3:04 am ☽ → ♈ 10:56 am	19 2nd ♈	20 2nd ♈ ☽ v/c 5:46 pm ☽ → ♉ 6:43 pm	21 2nd ♉
25 3rd ♊ ☽ v/c 12:31 am ☽ → ♋ 1:38 am	26 3rd ♋	27 3rd ♋ ☽ v/c 2:22 am ☽ → ♌ 3:35 am	28 3rd ♌
2	3	4	5

Eastern Daylight Time (EDT) becomes Eastern Standard Time (EST) November 4

Zodiac Signs

♈ Aries
♉ Taurus
♊ Gemini
♋ Cancer
♌ Leo
♍ Virgo
♎ Libra
♏ Scorpio
♐ Sagittarius
♑ Capricorn
♒ Aquarius
♓ Pisces

Planets

☉ Sun
☽ Moon
☿ Mercury
♀ Venus
♂ Mars
♃ Jupiter
♄ Saturn
♅ Uranus
♆ Neptune
♇ Pluto

NOVEMBER 2018

TH	F	SA	NOTES
4th ♌ **1**	4th ♌ **2** ☽ v/c 12:32 am ☽ → ♍ 1:48 am	4th ♍ **3**	
1st ♏ **8** ☽ v/c 5:42 am ☽ → ♐ 1:59 pm	1st ♐ **9**	1st ♐ **10** ☽ v/c 10:35 pm ☽ → ♑ 10:55 pm	
1st ♒ ◐ 2nd Quarter 9:54 am ☽ v/c 10:58 pm ☽ → ♓ 11:41 pm	2nd ♓ **16** ♀ D 5:51 am ☿ ℞ 8:33 pm *Venus direct* *Mercury retrograde*	2nd ♓ **17**	
2nd ♉ **22** ☉ → ♐ 4:01 am ☽ v/c 4:59 am ☽ → ♊ 11:10 pm *Thanksgiving Day* *Sun enters Sagittarius*	2nd ♊ ○ Full Moon 12:39 am *Mourning Moon*	3rd ♊ **24**	
3rd ♌ ◑ ☽ v/c 4:47 am ☽ → ♍ 6:08 am 4th Quarter 7:19 pm	4th ♍ **30**	1	
6	7	8	

Aspects & Moon Phases

☌ Conjunction	0°	● New Moon	(1st Quarter)
⚹ Sextile	60°	◐ Waxing Moon	(2nd Quarter)
□ Square	90°	○ Full Moon	(3rd Quarter)
△ Trine	120°	◑ Waning Moon	(4th Quarter)
⚻ Quincunx	150°		
☍ Opposition	180°		

DECEMBER 2018

SU	M	T	W
25	26	27	28
2 4th ♎	3 4th ♎ ☽ v/c 1:16 pm ☽ → ♏ 2:55 pm	4 4th ♏	5 4th ♏ ☽ v/c 4:53 pm ☽ → ♐ 9:49 pm
9 1st ♑	10 1st ♑ ☽ v/c 4:27 pm ☽ → ♒ 6:39 pm	11 1st ♒	12 1st ♒
16 2nd ♈	17 2nd ♈	18 2nd ♈ ☽ v/c 2:21 am ☽ → ♉ 4:37 am	19 2nd ♉ ☽ v/c 7:42 pm
23 3rd ♋	24 3rd ♋ ☽ v/c 9:50 am ☽ → ♌ 11:59 am *Christmas Eve*	25 3rd ♌ *Christmas Day*	26 3rd ♌ ☽ v/c 10:37 am ☽ → ♍ 12:50 pm
30 4th ♎ ☽ v/c 5:53 pm ☽ → ♏ 8:23 pm	31 4th ♏ *New Year's Eve*	1	2

Eastern Standard Time (EST)

Zodiac Signs

♈ Aries
♉ Taurus
♊ Gemini
♋ Cancer
♌ Leo
♍ Virgo
♎ Libra
♏ Scorpio
♐ Sagittarius
♑ Capricorn
♒ Aquarius
♓ Pisces

Planets

☉ Sun
☽ Moon
☿ Mercury
♀ Venus
♂ Mars
♃ Jupiter
♄ Saturn
♅ Uranus
♆ Neptune
♇ Pluto